NATIVE AMERICANS
OF THE SOUTHWEST

NATIVE AMERICANS OF THE SOUTHWEST

The Serious Traveler's Introduction to Peoples and Places

ZDENEK AND JOY M. SALZMANN

WestviewPress

A Division of HarperCollins*Publishers*

Frontispiece photo courtesy of Museum of Northern Arizona Photo Archives (E203B.36/83.0218). Photo by M. Middleton.

Copyright © 1997 by Westview Press, A Division of HarperCollins Publishers, Inc.

Published in 1997 in the United States of America by Westview Press, 5500 Central Avenue, Boulder, Colorado 80301-2877, and in the United Kingdom by Westview Press, 12 Hid's Copse Road, Cumnor Hill, Oxford OX2 9JJ

Library of Congress Cataloging-in-Publication Data
Salzmann, Zdenek.
    Native Americans of the Southwest : the serious traveler's
introduction to peoples and places / Zdenek and Joy M. Salzmann.
        p.   cm.
    Includes index.
    ISBN 0-8133-2279-0 (pb)
        1. Indians of North America—Southwest, New—Antiquities—
Guidebooks.   2. Indians of North America—Southwest, New—Material
culture—Guidebooks.   3. Indians of North America—Museums—
Southwest, New—Guidebooks.   4. Southwest, New—Description and
travel—Guidebooks.   5. Southwest, New—Antiquities—Guidebooks.
I. Salzmann, Joy M.   II. Title.
E78.S7S25   1997
917.904′053—dc21   97-701
                                                                    CIP

The paper used in this publication meets the requirements of the American National Standard for Permanence of Paper for Printed Library Materials Z39.48-1984.

10   9   8   7   6   5   4   3   2

CONTENTS

MAPS AND ILLUSTRATIONS

Maps

Photographs

PREFACE

Our intention in preparing this little book has been to provide visitors to the Southwest a concise guide to the Native Americans who live there and to their rich heritage. Because visitors come to the Southwest primarily to *see* rather than to *read about* the area, we have attempted to present the information we think may be of most interest in as few words as possible, a task we admit we found more than a little daunting.

Because many who come to the Southwest want to take back with them items the area is particularly known for, we have included a chapter on southwestern arts and crafts. For centuries Native Americans of this region have produced exquisite objects of many different types that are now valued as artwork. Making choices from among so many striking possibilities can be one of the particular pleasures of a visit here.

For those who expect to include in their plans some of the national monuments and parks containing fascinating architectural sites constructed centuries before Columbus touched the North American continent, we have included a chapter on prehistoric monuments in the Southwest. Detailed illustrated publications concerning these remarkable sites are available in each visitor center.

Those interested in museum exhibits concerning Native Americans will find a comprehensive listing of the many museums of the region in Appendix A, "Exhibits Relating to Native Americans of the Southwest." And for visitors who might like to see some of the traditional events, especially dances, held by Native Americans, we have compiled Appendix B, "Special Events," to provide help in determining dates, times, and locations.

We are indebted to several individuals who read either entire chapters or portions of chapters and then gave us the benefit of their expertise. They include anthropologists David A. Breternitz, Dena F. Dincauze, Christian E. Downum, Francis E. Smiley, Michael L. Vasquez, John J. Wood, Richard B. Woodbury, and Barton A. Wright. In addition we received valuable comments from Dan Garland of Sedona, Arizona, and a number of superintendents of national monuments and parks. We considered their comments very carefully and accepted many of their suggestions. Occasionally we were not able to make use of all their valuable comments because the text would have increased far beyond the original intent. Any errors of fact or omissions are ours alone.

We are also indebted to members of the editorial staff at Westview Press who gave us advice at various stages of the project—in particular, Dean Birkenkamp and those who saw the book through to completion: Jill Rothenberg, Lisa Wigutoff, Shena Redmond, and Marian Safran.

Finally, we wish visitors to the Southwest a fascinating journey through this magnificent part of the United States.

Zdenek Salzmann
Joy M. Salzmann

NATIVE AMERICANS
OF THE SOUTHWEST

1

 INTRODUCING
THE SOUTHWEST

Spectacular rock formations unmatched anywhere else in the world, steep-walled canyons, high mesas, trout streams in beautiful mountain settings, deserts alive with strange and fascinating cactuses and other plants that constantly catch the eye, night skies brimming over with stars—all these and more are waiting for the visitor to the Southwest. Arizona's Grand Canyon, perhaps the most spectacular natural wonder of the world, attracts visitors not only from all parts of this country but also from every area of the globe. According to an estimate made by the Tourism Research Library of Northern Arizona University, of the more than 26 million people who traveled to Arizona during 1994, 2.8 million were international visitors, most of them coming to the United States from Mexico, Canada, Germany, the United Kingdom, and Japan. Besides the Grand Canyon, there are many other natural features and prehistoric sites to see and be awed by: Zion and Bryce Canyons and Monument Valley in Utah; Mesa Verde in Colorado; Chaco Canyon and Carlsbad Caverns in New Mexico; and Lake Powell, with its hundreds of canyons easily accessible by boat, the Painted Desert, and Oak Creek Canyon in Arizona. Those are only a few of many dozens.

One of the features that make the Southwest different from the rest of the country—and for some perhaps even a bit exotic—is the active coexistence of a variety of cultures: Native American (the oldest cultures, and what this book will be about), Latino (dating back to the end of the 1500s, when

Spanish settlers came north from New Spain), and Anglo-American (the most recent, beginning in the 1800s; Arizona, the very last of the forty-eight contiguous states, achieved statehood only in 1912). Among the fifty states, New Mexico has the highest percentage of Latinos (some 35 percent), with Native Americans making up about 9 percent of the state's total population. In Arizona the figures are 15 percent for Latinos and 6 percent for Native Americans. What these figures indicate is that in New Mexico, for example, almost every other person is a Latino or Native American.

These groups keep alive their histories and their customs with colorful fiestas, powwows, religious ceremonies, historical celebrations and reenactments, and arts and crafts fairs that are full of vitality. Some of the distinctive crafts and art forms of the Native Americans are not only beautiful but also unique, not to be found elsewhere in the United States.

The Southwest—The Land

The definition of what makes up the U.S. Southwest as a region has changed in the course of U.S. history. After the Mexican War and the Treaty of Guadalupe Hidalgo in 1848, the term *Southwest* came to include Arizona and New Mexico and the adjacent parts of Nevada, Utah, Colorado, Oklahoma, and Texas. California has generally been excluded. No matter how the boundaries of what is considered the Southwest are drawn, Arizona and New Mexico make up its core.

What are some of the physical features that characterize the Southwest and make it a geographic area in its own right? We have already mentioned the unforgettable natural features of this part of the United States, but to emphasize high plateaus, deep canyons, deserts, and very dry climate does not mean that a variety of crops cannot be grown in the area. The Colorado River, the Rio Grande, and some of their tributaries provide water for irrigation, and several large dams help to control the flow of large volumes of water—Roosevelt Dam, Hoover (or Boulder) Dam, and Glen Canyon Dam.

A relief map of Arizona divides the state's land surface between the Colorado Plateau in the northeast and the Basin and

Range province in the west and south, with the transitional zone, or Central Highlands, separating them. Most of the elevations of the Colorado Plateau, which extends into the four states that come together at the Four Corners (Utah, Colorado, Arizona, and New Mexico), range between 5,000 and 8,000 feet. Humphreys Peak, one of the San Francisco Peaks just north of Flagstaff, reaches a height of 12,633 feet but can be climbed without any special mountaineering equipment.

The transitional zone, under the Mogollon Rim escarpments that slant diagonally across Arizona from northwest to southeast, also presents some rugged peaks as well as the spectacular scenery of Oak Creek Canyon and the surrounding Red Rock country. Millions of people have become acquainted with the beauty of this area by seeing such old-time Westerns as *Johnny Guitar,* with actors Sterling Hayden and Joan Crawford, *Broken Arrow,* with James Stewart, and *The Last Wagon,* with Richard Widmark.

Farther south and west the basin-and-range country consists of gentle valleys and open-ended basins, with occasional mountains rising above them. It is in the basins of the southern half of the state, at altitudes of about 2,000 to 5,000 feet, that the majority of Arizonans make their homes. This area includes Phoenix, the largest metropolitan area in the state, with a population of more than 2 million people. The Sonoran Desert, which lies in the southwestern part of the state and extends west and south into California and Mexico, is part of the basin-and-range country. It includes not only the Phoenix area but also Arizona's second largest city, Tucson, home of the world-famous Arizona–Sonora Desert Museum. In 1940 Tucson was a city of only 40,000 people, but today metropolitan Tucson's population is well above the half million mark.

Although winters on the Colorado Plateau tend to be cold, during the day the sun raises the temperature considerably. Because of the differences in elevation, temperatures in Flagstaff are usually about 25° to 30°F lower than those of Phoenix, about 140 miles to the south in the Sonoran, where daytime temperatures may reach as high as 120°F during the summer months. In general, the basin-and-range region is arid and semiarid, with occasional frosts during winter nights.

Although much of the plateau receives between 10 and 20 inches of precipitation annually, some of it must make do with less than 10. Southwestern Arizona also receives less than 10 inches, but several areas in the center of the state get from 20 to 30 inches, and the White Mountains in the east-central part of the state may receive even more. The summer monsoons, as they are called, bring short heavy thunderstorms to the state in July and August, but their onset and intensity vary from year to year.

The differences in temperatures and amount of precipitation account for the variety of Arizona's vegetation and animal life. Elevations 7,000 feet and higher favor ponderosa pine, Douglas fir, spruce, and aspen. Lower elevations feature piñon pine, juniper, and Gambel oak. The conditions of the southern portions of the state, including the Sonoran Desert area, favor mesquite and creosote bush. Cacti are to be found over the entire state, but the giant saguaro (as tall as 50 feet), organ-pipe cactus, and the Joshua tree (a species of yucca) are susceptible to frost and so prefer the southern or western parts of the state. Native grasses are important for the state's ranching industry.

The relatively low population density (about thirty times lower than that of New Jersey) and "wilderness" character of much of the state have helped to preserve habitat for some of the larger mammals such as bear, different species of deer, desert bighorn sheep, antelope, elk, javelina (wild pig), mountain lion, and coyote. Bird-watchers may catch sight of eagles and hawks as well as owls, ravens, roadrunners, quail, and humming-birds—again, to mention only a very few members of Arizona's large bird population. Of the plentiful reptiles and arachnids only a few are poisonous—Gila monsters, several species of rattlesnakes, scorpions, and black widow spiders among them—but most snakes and lizards are harmless, and tarantulas, although their appearance tends to frighten people, bite humans only when provoked, and their bites are not serious. Hiking and climbing should only be done in sturdy shoes. Hikers and climbers should never step or reach into places they cannot first check out by sight.

The topography of New Mexico, of which more than 85 percent is more than 4,000 feet above sea level, is also quite diversified. Geographers assign the topographical features of the state to four major systems: the northwest area to the Colorado Plateau, the north-central region to the southern Rocky Mountains, the central and southwestern parts to the Basin and Range province, and the approximately two fifths of the state that lie east of the Pecos River to the Great Plains. Most of New Mexico receives less than 20 inches of precipitation annually, with some areas getting less than 8; the highest elevations of the Rockies, however, may receive as much as 30, a great deal of it in the form of snow.

Just as in Arizona, temperatures in New Mexico vary with altitude, and humidity is generally quite low because much of the state lies within the semiarid and arid zones. Because the physical conditions are much like those of Arizona and the population density is even lower, New Mexico's diverse plant and animal life is similar to that of its western neighbor.

The state's most populous city is Albuquerque, whose metropolitan area population has reached the half million mark. Next in size is Santa Fe, the state capital, with a metropolitan population of more than 100,000 people. Not surprisingly in such a dry climate, most of the population centers have developed along rivers.

The geographic features of those parts of the adjoining states that make up the Southwest are similar to the adjacent areas of Arizona and New Mexico. Therefore they need not be described separately.

The Concepts of Culture and Society

Since this guide is anthropologically oriented, at the beginning it seems appropriate to make clear what anthropology is all about. Very simply, anthropology is the study of humankind. And because members of the human genus have been around more than two million years, spreading over the whole earth and managing to live successfully in even the most extreme environments, the study of humanity is necessarily a very large order. As a result, anthropology has come to be divided into four major subfields: (1) archaeology, the study of past cultures through the analysis of their material remains; (2) physical anthropology, the study of the origins and the biologically determined characteristics of the human species; (3) linguistic anthropology, the study of language and speech in the context of the culture and society that make use of them; and (4) cultural (or social) anthropology, the study of the lifestyles of different human societies.

Two terms that are frequently used when talking about Native Americans of the Southwest are *culture* (or *cultural*) and *society* (or *social*). In anthropology, *culture* takes in all human behavior that is learned (is not instinctive) and all its tangible and intangible results. In this sense, then, knocking on someone's door is just as much an instance of cultural behavior as a space walk. A can opener is as much a cultural product as a jet airliner. And planning a shower for someone about to be married is as much a cultural preoccupation as designing a radio telescope. Obviously, not all instances of learned behavior and its products are equally complex and important, but *all* are manifestations of culture. The concept of culture includes so much and can be viewed from so many vantage points that it has been redefined many times. Its two main characteristics are (1) that culture refers to *learned* patterns of behavior and (2) that it is *shared* by the members of a society. The term *society* refers to a human population (which can range in size from a hunting-and-gathering band to a large industrialized nation) characterized by common patterns of relationships and shared institutions. In short, the term *culture* emphasizes time depth, tradition, common values, and ways of living; the term *society* stresses the links and networks that join individuals and groups to other individuals and groups within a common framework.

The Southwest Culture Area

During their long prehistory and until early historic times, Native American societies displayed great cultural variety. But because particular natural environments called for special cultural adaptations, some societies within an area shared similar cultural orientations. Such areas are referred to in anthropology as culture areas. Among the dozen or so culture areas widely accepted for North America are the Arctic, Northwest Coast, Plateau, Great Basin, California, Plains (sometimes grouped together with the Prairies), Eastern Woodlands, and Southwest. Some of these culture areas are well known to the general public for their highly visible cultural features. The Northwest Coast is known for its impressive totem poles and the Plains for its expert horsemen, its tepees, and the sun dance. The Southwest has many characteristics of interest that differentiate it from the other North American culture areas.

Most anthropologists specializing in the study of Native Americans would define the Southwest culture area as including Arizona and New Mexico, southernmost Utah (south of the San Juan River), the extreme southwestern corner of Colorado, the extreme western and southern parts of Texas, and the southern tip of Nevada. (The Southwest culture area extends also into Mexico, but we are not concerned here with cultures below the border.)

Of the various Native American societies assigned to the Southwest culture area, many have distinctly different lifeways. What almost all of them have had in common, though, is the practice of agriculture, even long before they encountered the newcomers from Europe in the early sixteenth century. In some parts of the area, especially in river basins, farming was intensive. But even some of the peoples who were settled in high altitudes without year-round streams became true farmers. To overcome the aridity of the environment, some Native Americans constructed efficient irrigation canals. Among the original crops were corn, beans, and squash, supplemented when necessary with game and wild plants.

In addition to the older populations of the area, sometime after A.D. 1000 but before 1500 (probably closer to the latter date) the Navajo and the closely related Apache came to the Southwest from what today is west-central Canada. The Navajo learned to raise crops from their Pueblo neighbors but never became enthusiastic farmers. The Apache tended to remain hunters and gatherers.

Native American Languages of the Southwest

Visitors to the Southwest who are willing to explore the area by taking some of the less traveled roads are likely to hear a variety of languages besides English and Spanish. These are the languages of the Native American peoples who have made the Southwest their home. Many of these languages are quite different from one another. According to a conservative classification, the native languages still spoken in the Southwest belong to six different language families. (The term *language family* refers to all languages that are related by having descended over a long period of time from a single ancestral language. Some language families have quite a few member languages. The Indo-European family, for example, includes English and most of the languages spoken in Europe, several of which have spread to other parts of the world, as well as some languages spoken in southwestern Asia and India.)

The native language families found in the Southwest are Uto-Aztecan (for example, the Hopi language), Kiowa-Tanoan (the Santa Clara dialect of Tewa), Athapaskan (Navajo), Yuman (Havasupai), Keresan (the Acoma dialect of Keres, the only member of the family), and Zuni (unrelated to any other language and therefore another one-member language family).

Native American languages are sometimes referred to as "dialects," mainly by people who know little or nothing about the languages. These people think that Native American languages are "primitive" and somehow not full-fledged languages. For example, these languages are sometimes thought of as "primitive-sounding" simply because their sounds are different from those of English and can be difficult to pronounce. Another common misconception is that the languages of peoples whose societies are not urbanized and industrialized have "little grammar" and very limited vocabularies. Nothing could be farther from the truth.

Native American languages differ from English and from one another in their sounds just as the sounds of English differ from the sounds of Russian or Japanese. They all have distinct and just as intricate grammatical systems as the languages taught in American high schools and colleges. And their vocabularies efficiently handle all the subtle distinctions that communication among members of these societies requires. The languages within a language family differ from each other just as much as English differs from other members of the Indo-European languages such as Spanish, German, or Russian. And languages belonging to different language families—say, Hopi and Navajo—are just as strikingly different as English and Arabic or English and Japanese. To learn to speak one of these Native American languages well would require just as much effort and practice as learning to speak French or Spanish or Russian. To think of these languages as "primitive" is therefore not only disrespectful but contrary to the fact.

*   *   *

In the chapters that follow, we would like to acquaint visitors to the Southwest with the rich cultural heritage of the various Native American peoples who were in this fascinating region of the United States first and who still consider it their home. We will try to do so by sketching their prehistory and their relations with Europeans during the past 500 years of Southwestern history, and by giving the readers some idea of their traditional way of life and their present-day situation. And finally we will provide information as to the location of exhibits having to do with the material cultures of the Southwest as well as a listing of special Native American events that take place throughout the year.

2

PREHISTORY
OF THE SOUTHWEST

Prehistory is the study of humankind before events could be recorded in writing. In the American Southwest, prehistoric times ended in the mid-1500s when Coronado and his men explored the region. The presence of Native Americans, however, preceded the entry of European explorers in the area by many thousands of years. When and from where did these original immigrants come to the New World?

Who Discovered America?

America was not discovered by the Norse mariner Leif Eriksson, who is believed to have touched the northeastern coast of North America around the year 1000, nor even 500 years later by Christopher Columbus, Amerigo Vespucci, or other European navigators and explorers. Many thousands of years earlier it was discovered by the ancestors of today's Native Americans. These very first immigrants entered the New World by crossing the strip of land connecting northeastern Siberia and Alaska.

Today the Bering Strait, which separates the Bering Sea from the Arctic Ocean, is about 60 miles wide at its narrowest point, and although it is not very deep (less than 300 feet at its deepest), it would not have been easily crossable with a primitive vessel. However, when the most recent glacial period in North America was at its highest point, so much water had been withdrawn from the seas and locked in massive glaciers that the first immigrants could have crossed the Bering Strait on dry land, known as the Bering land bridge. The floor of the strait was repeatedly exposed between about 60,000 and 15,000 years ago. In addition, the water in the strait would at times have been frozen solidly enough to support humans and animals. It had been assumed that once the strait was behind them, the first immigrants could have made use of a narrow corridor that led south between huge ice walls into the warmer part of the continent. But a very recent reconstruction of the prehistoric ecology of this ice-free corridor makes a good case for the corridor to have been unusable until about 12,000 years ago.

When Did the First People Enter the New World?

On this question, anthropologists are not in complete agreement. Some of them believe that the arrival of the first Americans could not have occurred much earlier than about 12,000 years ago. Others hold that the initial waves of migration from northeast Asia must have begun a long time before that, perhaps as early as 50,000 or so years ago. How can there be so widely differing opinions among students of prehistory? The lack of agreement has to do with the nature and interpretation of archaeological evidence.

The assumption that the peopling of the Americas is of relatively recent date—some 12,000 years ago—is based on the distribution of leaf-shaped flint projectile points with fluted faces, that is, with rounded longitudinal grooves on both sides to improve their hafting to spear shafts. These are known as Clovis points, named for Clovis, New Mexico, near which the first such points were discovered. Associated with bones of large prehistoric mammals, these points were found widely distributed over much of North America in sites that have been dated to as early as 11,500 years ago. Because at present they are the oldest indisputably human-made artifacts in the New World, some anthropologists believe that the first people to arrive in this continent could not have preceded the users of these points by a very long period of time.

But according to other anthropologists, some evidence exists to indicate that human presence in the Americas could have preceded the Clovis culture by several thousand years. In support of this claim they point, for example, to the Meadowcroft rock shelter near the Ohio River west of Pittsburgh. The sediment accumulated on the floor of the shelter was found to be over 17 feet deep and consisted of ten distinct layers, all showing evidence of human habitation. The oldest date established for the items of material culture found there, using the carbon-14 method of dating, is about 12,000 to 14,000 years ago. Another site with evidence suggesting that the Clovis culture was not the earliest one is Monte Verde in southern Chile. There archaeologists found wood, mastodon bones, charcoal, a variety of plant remains (including wild potatoes), and stone tools. The radiocarbon dates for Monte Verde are 12,500 to 13,000 years ago, but with Monte Verde's location so far to the south, it would seem likely that the ancestors of those who established the settlement crossed the Bering land bridge several thousand years earlier.

Sites exist in the Americas that may be still older than the ones mentioned. For one site in northeastern Brazil the claim has been made that what a few archaeologists believe to be hearths and crude stone tools go back some 30,000 years. Although the carbon-14 method of dating has become a reliable means of dating organic archaeological materials up to about 70,000 years, it is frequently difficult or even impossible to determine, for example, whether a piece of charcoal comes from the remains of a human-originated fire or from a tree ignited by lightning.

The position that humans may have been in the Americas longer than 12,000 years also receives some support from linguistic evidence. It is fair to assume that not a great many different languages were spoken in northeastern Asia at the time the ancestors of Native Americans were filtering into the New World. But over the period during which humans inhabited the Americas, the continents became very highly differentiated linguistically, with at least 150 different language families and more than 1,000 individual languages. Such a high degree of differentiation could scarcely have come about in only 10,000 or so years.

It seems reasonable to discard the possibility that the first immigrants into the Americas arrived by way of the Pacific Ocean. No evidence exists to indicate that even 12,000 to 15,000 years ago Asians possessed watercraft capable of making such a journey. But even if some transpacific contacts between the Old World and the New prior to 1492 were to be accepted, the migration of large numbers of people over the Bering Strait is not questioned by any anthropologist.

The first immigrants into the New World were physically fully modern, belonging to the same subspecies—*Homo sapiens sapiens*—that all modern humans have belonged to for tens of thousands of years. Although the cultures of the first Americans were materially simple, just like the cultures of other peoples at the time, these early Americans must have been accomplished hunters of large game, and they made ingenious adjustments to the wide variety of environments they found in the New World.

The position that humans have been in the New World for only about 12,000 years may yet prove to be somewhat conservative. What most anthropologists agree on, however, is that initially the immigrants from Asia must have been attracted to the new continent in pursuit of game, and that their arrival was not a single massive population shift across the Bering Strait but the result of migrations by small bands over a long period of time, quite possibly extending over several thousand years.

Prehistory—The Early Period

The earliest archaeologically documented human occupation of the Southwest dates back to at least 11,000 B.P. (before the present—this is the usual way archaeologists now indicate prehistoric dates, in this case, 9000 B.C.). Just as in other parts of North America, these early people were big-game hunters who moved about from place to place in small bands. They were skilled in producing finely crafted projectile points and other stone tools with which they were able to kill large game and also to process hides and bones as well as wood. The animals that roamed the Southwest, at that time a well-watered grassland with forested higher elevations, were impressive in both variety and number. They included mammoths, bison, horses, camels, and giant sloths as well as the dire wolves and great cats that were their predators. Between about 10,000 and 7000 B.P. many of these species became extinct. One likely reason would have been the drying up of the grassland areas, but the efficient hunting techniques of the ancient Americans were likely also a contributing factor. In any case, by about 7000 B.P. physical conditions in the Southwest must have already become much like those of today.

With most of the large mammals gone, the inhabitants of the area had to resort to hunting whatever smaller game they could find—bighorn sheep, mule and white-tailed deer, but also rabbits, birds, and small rodents. They would also have needed to intensify their gathering of wild plants and collecting of seeds. What ultimately contributed to changes in the subsistence patterns of the early inhabitants of the Southwest was the introduction of cultivated crops. Corn (maize) made its way into the Southwest from what is now Mexico close to 3000 B.P. The cultivation of squash may go back almost as far. Beans were not grown until much later, about A.D. 800 to 900. As important as the introduction of domesticated plants was to the Southwest, for many centuries the harvests may have been so small that hunting and gathering would have remained a necessary means of obtaining additional food.

The full significance of farming had to wait until the final centuries B.C. Because the ability to grow plants and harvest them year after year makes permanent settlements possible, the development of the many villages for which the Southwest is so well known was the eventual result of the development of farming. Little evidence of permanent settlements has been found dating earlier than about 800 B.C., but from that time on their number steadily increased. The earliest use of pottery dates back to about A.D. 200. People made and used pottery over a widespread area from the southern deserts to the northern portions of the Colorado Plateau. Because clay pots in large numbers cannot easily be carried, their use is invariably associated with the storage of foodstuffs resulting from the harvesting of domesticated plants, as well as with cooking and water collecting. It is safe to say that pottery, too, made its way to the Southwest from Mexico, where it had appeared at about the time that agriculture was becoming established there several thousand years earlier.

Over the course of time, four major prehistoric cultural traditions became identifiable in the Southwest—Mogollon, Hohokam, Anasazi (Ancestral, or early, Puebloan), and Hakataya. All

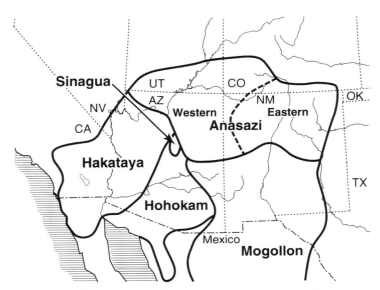

Approximate boundaries of the main prehistoric cultures of the Southwest. Over the centuries boundaries have changed or overlapped to varying degrees.

four developed from regional variants of the widespread Desert culture that preceded them.

The Mogollon

The Mogollon area (named after the Mogollon Mountains in southwestern New Mexico) includes some of southeastern Arizona and most of southern New Mexico, as well as the adjacent parts of Texas and of Sonora and Chihuahua, Mexico. The period of the Mogollon culture began around A.D. 200–300 and lasted until about a century before Coronado's explorations in the 1500s. Archaeologists have been able to learn a great deal about the way of life of the Mogollon people. Their earliest villages, built in high locations for protection, were small and consisted of subterranean pit houses. These dwellings were dug several feet into the ground—which makes for good insulation both winter and summer—and were roofed over with poles, brush, and earth. The ancestors of the Mogollon people, the earliest farmers of the Southwest, had learned to cultivate maize, squash, and beans from the Native Americans to the south of them. Grinding corn with handheld manos (stones used as upper millstones) on metates (large flat or troughed slabs) was also a practice continued from the earlier Desert culture. The modest crops of the Mogollon people were supplemented by hunting, fishing, and the gathering of wild plant food (for example, piñon nuts, walnuts, prickly pear cactus, acorns, and sunflower seeds).

The Mogollon were among the earliest pottery makers in the Southwest. They decorated their pitchers, jars, and bowls with geometrical figures and later with stylized animal figures (insects, fish, frogs, birds, rabbits, deer, mountain sheep, and humans). The people wore bracelets, rings, and pendants of shell obtained through trade; made fiber sandals; produced coiled and twined baskets; played on reed flutes; and hunted with spears, darts, and, later, bows and arrows.

The Mogollon culture progressed through several phases during its 1,500-year existence. From about A.D. 500 to 700 few crops were cultivated and dependence on wild foods increased considerably. Archaeologists still don't understand why this shift occurred.

The Hohokam

On a contemporary map of Arizona, the center of the Hohokam culture would be just a little east of where Phoenix is now located, with the culture's northernmost extension reaching to an area near Flagstaff and its southernmost to the U.S.-Mexican border area southwest of Tucson. Hohokam culture lasted from about A.D. 200 to the mid-1400s (the name Hohokam comes from a Pima or Papago word meaning "those who have gone"). The dwellings of these people were first of wattle-and-daub construction and later of adobe. The Hohokam were also makers of good pottery and some interesting ceramic figurines, most of which represented the female human form. From shells that they obtained from the Gulf of California and the Pacific through trade, and possibly even from collecting trips of their own, they made beads, rings, mosaic plaques, bracelets, and pendants, some of which were shaped like snakes, frogs, or birds. But the Hohokam were perhaps best known for the canals they built to bring water to irrigate their fields from rivers as much as 30 miles away. Their main crop was corn, but they also cultivated beans, squash, bottle gourds, and cotton. Their ball courts and platform mounds show the influence of Native American cultures from Mesoamerica and were also undoubtedly used for ceremonial purposes. In fact, the similarities are so striking that some archaeologists believe that the first Hohokam migrated northward from Mesoamerica.

Some archaeologists have used the name O'otam, meaning "person, human being" in the Pima language, to refer to the prehistoric ancestors of the Piman-speaking groups, today's Pimas and Tohono O'odham (Papagos), who reside in south-central and southern Arizona and northern Mexico. The prehistoric area of this culture included parts of southern Arizona and the adjacent parts of Mexico, including an elongated extension to the south. During the early centuries of the Christian era, the O'otam lived in crude pit houses in small, loosely organized villages and engaged in seasonal dry farming and pottery making. Although the archaeological record is not yet sufficient to understand the prehistory of these people in detail, it appears that they were in contact with various other southwestern cultures. Between the eleventh and fourteenth centuries, they were intruded upon by a people settled east of them in what today is northwestern Chihuahua (Mexico), and in the mid-fifteenth century they were in contact at least marginally even with the Anasazi (Ancestral Puebloan peoples). The borrowings from these contacts included large ceramic receptacles, ball courts, ornaments made of shell and copper, walled adobe villages, and eventually stone architecture of the Puebloan type.

The Ancestral Puebloans (Anasazi)

North of the Mogollon and Hohokam peoples were the Ancestral Puebloans, or Anasazi, from a Navajo word meaning "alien," or "enemy ancestors." (Because of the meaning of the word, Native Americans as well as archaeologists now prefer to refer to these prehistoric inhabitants of the northern part of the Southwest as "early" or "ancestral" Puebloans [Pueblos]. Since the word *Anasazi* has been used in the literature and in museum exhibits for some 60 years, we will use the term at least parenthetically.) By about A.D. 1200 the area of the early Puebloan culture extended over the northeastern third of Arizona, the northwestern third of New Mexico, and, to the north, the adjoining parts of Utah and Colorado.

To begin with, the Ancestral Pueblo peoples were hunter-gatherers, but by about 3,000 years ago they were cultivating corn, squash, and beans, and supplementing their crops with game, wild plants, seeds, and piñon nuts. They became expert basket makers, weaving a variety of trays, bowls, storage trunks, and conical water baskets from yucca and other fibers. This is why archaeologists call the earlier period of their tradition Basket Maker stages II and III. (The designation Basket Maker I, referring to the preagricultural stage, is no longer used; it related to the transitional period between the Desert and Ancestral Puebloan cultures.)

Although during Basket Maker II (from about 1000 B.C. to A.D. 400) the early Puebloan peoples began farming, the yields from their fields were so modest that they still needed to hunt and gather in order to supplement their crops. They made use of spear-throwers to hunt deer and mountain sheep, increasing the power and range of their spears. The people lived in shelters built in caves or on heights that permitted them to look out over the land below. During the next three centuries, the Basket Maker III stage, they learned to make pottery and began to construct pit or slab houses (pit houses lined with stone slabs), but their subsistence still depended to some extent on hunting and gathering. Before the end of this period the more accurate bow and arrow had apparently replaced the spear and spear-thrower.

The period that followed the Basket Maker culture is divided into several stages called Pueblo because by that time the most characteristic feature of the culture was the pueblo, a settlement made up of adjoining rectangular dwellings built of stone and adobe. These structures were not only large enough to contain several rooms but also were built so expertly that multistoried houses were possible. During the Pueblo II and III stages (from about A.D. 900 to 1100 and from 1100 to 1300) these villages grew steadily in size and their inhabitants became specialized and accomplished artists and craftspeople.

The best-known pueblo of these early people is the so-called Cliff Palace, which was built into a large recess of a cliff wall in what is now Mesa Verde National Park in southwestern Colorado. Occupied from about A.D. 1100 to 1275, the pueblo contained more than 200 rooms, 23 kivas (ceremonial structures, usually round and partly underground), and numerous small storage areas. Toward the end of the thirteenth century, occupation of the Cliff Palace was discontinued—very likely as the result of an ecological crisis in which not only an extended drought but also soil erosion and deforestation played a part.

After 1300 the area occupied by the early Puebloans shrank to the valleys of the Little Colorado and the northern reaches of the Rio Grande, where the water supply was more reliable. The migration of these people away from the San Juan River and other areas in the north to more hospitable environments resulted in the development of fewer but larger communities, and the people may have been experiencing pressure from nomadic peoples coming into the Southwest from the north. In short, this last prehistoric period, Pueblo IV, from about A.D. 1300 to the Spanish conquest in the mid-1500s, must have been a time of stress for the Ancestral Puebloan (Anasazi) culture.

The Hakataya (Patayan)

The Hakataya (the name is based on a Yuman word for the Colorado River) occupied what today is west-central Arizona, the northern part of Baja California, southeast California, and the southern tip of Nevada. The material culture of the Hakataya (also referred to as Patayan) varied regionally not only because of its adaptation to different environments but also because it borrowed cultural traits from several neighboring groups. Relatively few Hakataya sites have been excavated compared to the number of sites of the Mogollon, Hohokam, and early Puebloans. We do know, however, that because the Hakataya practiced only marginal agriculture, they also needed to hunt and gather and as a result occasionally moved from place to place. For shelters they preferred to build circular huts with thatched roofs and walls constructed of poles or sticks that were then covered with clay or mud. They made crude stone tools and plain pottery, and used stone-lined pits for roasting food.

The Sinagua

Even though on the map the late prehistoric cultures of the Southwest appear to be separated from one another by sharp boundaries, some overlapping did occur. The most outstanding example of such blending is the Sinagua culture of central Arizona. The name Sinagua ("without water" in Spanish, referring to scarcity of surface water) has been used for these people by archaeologists to describe their dry-land farming techniques. The earliest sites of the Sinagua, dating from about the eighth century, were located in the vicinity of today's Flagstaff. These people, too, were agriculturalists, cultivating corn, beans, squash, gourds, and cotton. They made baskets and produced ornaments from stone, shell, turquoise, and red argillite.

Over the centuries the Sinagua were much influenced by the cultures of their various neighbors. For example, from the Hohokam they adopted living in sedentary sites, irrigating their fields, and constructing ball courts for ceremonial games; from the Ancestral Puebloans they learned to build masonry pueblos; and from them, the Mogollon, and the Hohokam they learned to produce several different types of pottery.

Sinagua culture peaked around the middle of the twelfth century, about a century after the eruptions in the mid-1060s of Sunset Crater near Flagstaff. The people who resettled in the area when it appeared to be safe to return found that the layers of cinders and volcanic ash held water in the soil, considerably increasing the yields of their crops. For reasons probably similar to those that caused the early Puebloans to leave their northern outposts, most of the Sinagua were gone from the Flagstaff area by about A.D. 1300, but they persisted for another century at lower elevations in the Verde River valley, a short distance to the south.

*   *   *

Of special importance to the Southwestern peoples were the cultures that had developed south of them in what today is Mexico. These civilizations influenced not only aspects of Southwestern material culture—agricultural practices, pottery, and architecture—but also religious beliefs and their attendant rituals. Some scholars have suggested that the Pueblo peoples' beliefs and practices concerning the katsinas, for example, may have derived originally from Aztec rain god cults. The blending of local Southwestern cultures with cultural elements elaborated earlier in the societies to the south, as well as the many prehistoric sites and monuments that the ancestors of today's Native Americans left behind, have made the area's prehistory of great interest not only to archaeologists but also to Southwest residents and visitors.

3

THE PUEBLOS

The Pueblo peoples of the Southwest have lived in villages for many centuries. They are the descendants of the prehistoric Anasazi and Mogollon peoples, whose traditional cultures included growing maize, beans, and squash, making basketry and pottery, and performing the elaborate ceremonies that supported their religious beliefs. (For the period before the arrival of the Spaniards, see Chapter 2.)

The Western Pueblos, who established their settlements in the mesa and canyon country, include the inhabitants of the Hopi villages and one Tewa village in northeastern Arizona, and also the Zuni, Acoma, and Laguna peoples of west-central New Mexico. The Eastern Pueblos—more than a dozen different peoples—live along the upper Rio Grande and its tributaries and include the villages of Taos, Santa Clara, Nambe, and San Ildefonso. Although all Pueblo peoples had much in common culturally before the arrival of Europeans, the impact of Spanish and later of Anglo-American culture was not so strongly felt by those in the Western Pueblo region, and the native peoples there were able to retain their traditional lifeways to a greater extent, especially the Hopi, than those in the east. But even the Eastern Pueblos managed to preserve many of their traditions by keeping them secret while outwardly "accepting" the Spanish government's administration and Catholic religion.

In our brief description of Western Pueblo societies we move from west to east. We start with the Hopi of northeastern Arizona.

The Hopi

The Hopi have lived in northeastern Arizona in what is known as Hopi country for at least 1,500 years. The village of Oraibi (frequently referred to as Old Oraibi) has been occupied since about A.D. 1100, and it vies with Acoma and Taos in New Mexico in claiming to be the oldest continuously inhabited community north of Mexico. Beginning about the fourteenth century, the Hopi villages became one of the centers of Pueblo life. Among the achievements of the Hopi—long before they encountered the Spaniards—was their highly specialized agriculture, making superb use of dry farming techniques in a climate and environment that does not favor the growing of crops. Precipitation is minimal, and there are no permanent or even semipermanent streams of water, though some springs do exist.

Worthy of note, too, is that from the thirteenth through the seventeenth century the Hopi extracted coal from beds cropping out not far below the tops of Hopi-country mesas. Removing the material overlying the coal deposits was difficult work, but coal could be used for heating, cooking, and firing pottery and so was very much worth the effort. The burros and iron axes the Spaniards introduced made it easier to gather wood than to extract coal, and by that time, too, the supply of easily reachable coal may have been nearly exhausted.

Most of the Hopi live on three mesas referred to—moving from east to west—as First Mesa, Second Mesa, and Third Mesa. The word *mesa,* meaning "table" in Spanish, is used in the Southwest to designate a flat-topped elevation with steeply sloping sides. In addition to the villages on each of the three mesas, several villages have sprung up below the mesas. The westernmost village, Moenkopi, is off the Hopi Reservation, a few miles southeast of Tuba City. The easternmost, Polacca, located just under First Mesa, is about 50 miles east of Moenkopi as the crow flies. Hano, a village on First Mesa, appears to be a typical Hopi village but is much more recent and of different ethnic and linguistic origin. Hano is a Tewa Indian community founded in 1700. According to Tewa oral history, the ancestors of these Tewas moved to First Mesa from what is now north-central New Mexico at the request of the clan chiefs of the First Mesa village of Walpi. The Hopi wanted the Tewa to help guard the mesa against invaders, apparently not only the Spaniards but non-Pueblo Indian raiders as well.

Historical Background

In 1598 an expedition of soldiers, colonists, and friars led by the Spaniard Juan de Oñate reached the valley of the upper Rio Grande. The purpose of this expedition was to Christianize the Native American villages of the Southwest and to colonize the Pueblo country for Spain. Even before that first year was over, the villagers of Acoma rebelled against the harsh measures imposed by the Spaniards. Severe punishment followed. The village was burned, hundreds of its inhabitants killed, and many additional hundreds taken captive and enslaved. But Oñate's success was limited. Most members of his expedition soon became disillusioned, and while their leader was on an exploratory trip to the northeast they returned to Chihuahua.

A new wave of missionary activity began after 1610, and between 1629 and 1641 three missions and two chapels were established in the Hopi villages, one mission in the easternmost village of Awatovi. But the Pueblos were still being brutally dealt with by the Spanish colonists, the soldiers, and even the clergy. Conditions became so harsh that in 1655 the Hopi felt compelled to send a delegation to Santa Fe, the seat of the Spanish governor. Its mission was to denounce a priest for publicly whipping a Hopi and then setting him afire for "an act of idolatry." The increasing hardships imposed upon the Pueblo peoples culminated in the Pueblo Revolt of 1680. In the Hopi villages alone, five priests were killed and their churches destroyed. In general the revolt was successful throughout the Southwest because, for once, all the Pueblo peoples had united in action.

But Pueblo peoples' freedom from Spanish oppression did not last long. In 1692 the Spaniards began the reconquest of the area. Some of the villages submitted without a struggle, but others resisted vigorously. What worked against the Native Americans this time was their strong tradition of village autonomy and the consequent lack of a unified effort against this second Spanish conquest. When in 1699 the Hopi of Awatovi permitted the Franciscans to return and even offered to rebuild their mission, the usually peaceful Hopi from other villages attacked the pueblo, killed the Awatovi men who resisted, and forced the women and children to leave their homes and move to other villages. Awatovi ceased to exist.

Over the years several military expeditions were dispatched to Hopi country to bring the villages under control—the first one in 1701 as punishment for the destruction of Awatovi. All these expeditions failed because of the easily defensible location of the villages on the tops of mesas. Repeated attempts by the priests to Christianize the Hopi were also unsuccessful. Except for a few individuals, the Hopi have retained many of their centuries-old religious beliefs and practices to the present day. During the 25 or so years that Pueblo country was on the northern frontier of a newly independent Mexico, the pressures on the Hopi were minimal, except for occasional raids by the Utes and the Navajo. Even after 1848, when the Hopi came under the jurisdiction of the United States, their relative isolation on the mesas, surrounded by the Navajo Reservation, helped them to preserve their traditional culture to a greater extent than perhaps any other Native Americans in North America.

The Past Hundred Years

The Hopi share a distinctive lifestyle and language, even though traditionally they lacked a centralized political organization. Instead, Hopi political life has been characterized by factionalism that at times has resulted in serious disruption to village life. During the fourth quarter of the nineteenth century, for example, Oraibi's population split between a conservative faction hostile to the U.S. government ("Hostiles") and a liberal faction that was friendly to it ("Friendlies"). When in 1906 the leader of the conservative faction invited some Hopis from Second Mesa to settle in Oraibi, a fight ensued between the conservatives and the liberals. The disagreement between the two factions of the village was so intense that the conservatives left Oraibi and founded a new village, Hotevilla, only a few miles to the northwest. When a year later some of the dissidents tried to return to Oraibi but were refused permission, they built the village of Bacabi (also spelled Bacavi) just across the road from Hotevilla. (We have given here the conventional version of the Oraibi split—an interpretation that is necessarily simplified.)

On the whole, then, the villages have each remained self-governing even though a constitution was drawn up for the Hopi in 1936 under the provisions of the Indian Reorganization Act passed two years earlier. This act was designed to bring about the formation of tribal councils that would represent entire reservations and would also deal with the federal government. In the case of the Hopi villages, a tribal council was organized, dissolved after several years, and later reorganized. But the individual villages prefer to retain as much autonomy in internal affairs as possible. The division between the "conservatives," or traditionalists, and the "liberals," or council supporters, has continued. The traditionalists are against the economic exploitation of the land and its resources, and in general want to minimize any influences from the outside that might undermine Hopi cultural sovereignty.

Despite the desire of the Hopi to preserve their traditional culture and to withstand the pressures of the Anglo-American society that surrounds them, some inevitable changes have taken place, especially since World War II. The Hopi have been increasingly exposed to the outside world, and as a result demand has developed for many consumer products. Once the main roads on the Hopi and Navajo reservations were paved, the villages became readily accessible by automobile. As a consequence, the Hopi mesas have become of so much interest to outsiders that at various ceremonial occasions large numbers of spectators crowd the village plazas. Unfortunately, some of the visitors have shown so little respect for the ritual activities that several villages are considering closing these events to outsiders.

As among the other Pueblos, the maternal line has been the traditional line of descent for the Hopi. Villages are divided into several subdivisions. Each subdivision is made up of several clans usually named for and linked with a particular animal or plant. Members of the same village subdivision are forbidden to marry each other. After marriage, a Hopi bridegroom goes to live with his wife in the house of her mother. The women are considered to be the owners of the houses and cultivable land. The typical Hopi household used to be made up of the members of an extended family and included an older woman and her husband, one or more of her daughters and their husbands and children, and any of her unmarried children. But for some years now, many young couples have preferred to establish a household of their own.

All Pueblo societies have always carried on a rich ceremonial life, and the Hopi are no exception. The ever-present possibility that the crops could fail for lack of rain has focused Hopi culture on the need for supernatural help. The Hopi venerate a large number of supernaturals—among them the sun, the earth, the god of death, the star god, Spider Woman, various mythical heroes, and some 300 katsinas. (More about the kachina dolls that represent the katsinas can be found in Chapter 5.)

The ceremonial calendar runs throughout the entire year and is designed to secure rain, a plentiful harvest, good health, and peace. Each village organizes its own ceremonies. Masked dancers representing the katsinas perform at the ceremonials of the first half of the year. The best-known ceremony of the latter part of the year is the Snake Dance. On the ninth day of the dance, in the village plaza, members of the Snake Society perform holding snakes—both harmless and poisonous—in their mouths. At the end of the ceremony the snakes are released in sacred places outside the village so that they can return to the gods and ask them for rain. Today the Snake Dance is held in only one village and for some years now has been closed to outsiders. Some of the very elaborate ceremonies, or parts of them, attract large audiences from the outside. Others are held in kivas, rectangular and partly underground structures.

Each village has several kivas. For the ceremonies held in the kivas temporary altars decorated with paintings of corn, clouds, lightning, and a variety of other sacred and mythological subjects are erected, and materials needed for the ceremony (such as prayer sticks and sacred cornmeal) are prepared. Praying, singing, dancing, and ritual smoking of native tobacco from a circulating pipe make up these ceremonies. Smoking is of great importance because smoke is thought to attract rain clouds. One of the most significant ceremonies performed in kivas is the initiation of adolescent boys into adult life. Although kivas are the ceremonial structures of the Hopi, they are also used as men's workshops.

Ceremonial activities are part of everyday life among the Pueblos, particularly among the Western Pueblo. Bringing about rain is only one of their objectives. The overall purpose of cere-

monialism is to ensure a harmonious balance at all times between the group and the world of nature and the supernatural.

A Note About the Tewa Village of First Mesa

The three centuries of sharing First Mesa with the Hopi has had
an effect on the culture of the Tewa. Some fundamental features
of ceremonial and social organizations in Hano, the Tewa village there, still resemble those of the New Mexico Tewa (for example, ceremonies that emphasize curing rather than rain and
fertility), but there are also features that were borrowed from
the Hopi. Regardless of origin, the various elements of both
their social structure and their ceremonialism have become well
integrated. The high incidence of intermarriage between the
Tewa and the Hopi has helped the blending process.

According to one observer, an anthropologist whose mother
was a Santa Clara Tewa, there is a noticeable difference in the
personality traits between the Tewa of Hano and their Hopi
neighbors. As he saw it, the Tewa were more practical and out-
going and therefore more adaptable to the larger American society around them.

The Zuni

The Zuni Reservation is located in western New Mexico southwest of what are called the Zuni Mountains. The western
boundaries of the reservation coincide with the border between
New Mexico and Arizona. In addition, the reservation includes
three small tracts of land—one in New Mexico south of the
main reservation and two in Arizona near the confluence of the
Zuni and Little Colorado Rivers. In 1990, the Zuni were
granted an easement along a pilgrimage trail, making it possible
for them to cross private land lying between the main reservation and the sacred area in Arizona where the Zuni people are
believed to reside after death. The total reservation area is just
over 650 square miles. Archaeological evidence of the occupation of what is now Zuni country goes back to about A.D. 700,
and ancestors of the present-day Zunis must have lived in the
area for at least several centuries before they came into contact

with the Spaniards in the mid-1500s. At that time the Zunis lived in six or seven villages, or pueblos. One of these villages was reported to have as many as 1,000 rooms, on three levels. It must have held a sizable population for its time.

Historical Background

Violence marked the Zuni's first contact with Europeans coming from New Spain, today's Mexico. One of the Zuni villages, Hawikuh, was attacked and taken over on July 7, 1540, by soldiers led by Francisco Vásquez de Coronado, who thought he had located the legendary seven cities of Cibola. They were thought to contain vast treasures, gold in particular. According to the expedition's chronicler, it was a great disappointment to Coronado and his men that they found nothing but "a little, crowded village."

The first Catholic mission to the Zuni was founded in 1629. Relations between the villagers and the three Spanish friars and the three soldiers who escorted them must have been tense, because in less than three years two priests and their escorts were killed. Then in 1680 the Zuni participated in the widespread Pueblo uprising against the Spaniards, both settlers and priests. Out of fear of eventual retribution, the Zuni moved out of their villages to defensible mesa tops, especially to the sacred mesa popularly called Corn Mountain, the traditional refuge of the Zuni. After Spanish control was reestablished in 1692, the Zuni descended from Corn Mountain. They chose to resettle only one of their previous villages—one that, although not easily defensible, had both spring water and a river nearby, making the land suitable for irrigated farming. That village is the one today called Zuni.

There the Spanish reestablished their mission. It functioned until 1821, when its operations stopped because of persistent Zuni resistance to being converted to Christianity and also because of the continuing threat of Apache and Navajo raids on the Southwestern pueblos. As early as 1672 or 1673 the Apaches had attacked Hawikuh, killed a priest and about 200 Zunis, taken 1,000 captive, stolen all the livestock, and burned the town.

During the Mexican period, between 1821 and the 1840s, visitors to Zuni were few, but soon after the discovery of gold in

California in 1848, the Zuni had to cope both with Navajo and Apache raiders and with Anglos on their way to California from the East, some of whom helped themselves to both the crops and the livestock of the Zuni. But by the end of the century not only were Anglo missionaries and government officials living and working in Zuni but teachers and traders as well. In 1879 the first anthropological expedition was sent to Zuni by John Wesley Powell, made famous by his journey down the Colorado River through the Grand Canyon and by this time director of the Bureau of Ethnology in Washington. One member of the expedition remained behind in Zuni when the others left, and he not only learned the language but eventually won both admission to the Society of Bow Priests and appointment as First War Chief. With the decline in warfare and the increasing influence of outsiders on the life of the pueblo, the prestige of warriors waned.

The Past Hundred Years

Zuni political organization, too, underwent changes. For example, during the 1880s the Bow Priests decided each year who should be members of the tribal council. Since the mid-1930s the council has been elected by secret ballot. The office insignia are a set of canes given to the Zuni by President Abraham Lincoln in 1863.

Although more and more Zunis have taken active interest in the larger society around them—several hundred men served in World War II and many young Zunis who have gone to college since then have not returned to the pueblo—they have managed to retain much of their traditional social and religious system. It consists of four subsystems that interlock and support each other: clans, kiva groups, curing societies, and priesthoods.

Members of clans trace their descent through the maternal line and do not marry a person from the same clan. The clans bear the names of the ancestors from whom Zunis trace their descent—Dogwood, Eagle, Sun, Badger, Turkey, Corn, Frog, Coyote, and others. Large clans divide into subclans. The clan system changes greatly over time, and during the past 100 years nine clans have become inactive or extinct. All boys between the ages of 8 and 12 undergo an initiation into one of the six kiva groups associated with the katsinas. The choice of a child's kiva group is made by a parent when the child is born, but a change later to another kiva group is not difficult. Membership in any one of the twelve curing societies is open to individuals of either sex. Membership in the Society of Bow Priests is limited to men, but Rain Priesthood members may be of either sex. The sometimes secret, sometimes public, ceremonies performed throughout the year by these two priesthoods are meant to ensure the well-being of the tribe. A major event of the ceremonial calendar is the masked Shalako ceremony held yearly in late November or early December. During this ceremony Zuni priests celebrate the annual coming of the supernaturals (katsinas) to the village and plant feathered prayer sticks to ensure the general prosperity of the villagers.

The basic economic unit among the Zuni is the household. Women tend to dominate in economic affairs, and whatever property a couple may accumulate belongs to the female. Unemployment or underemployment has been common despite a variety of sources of income. A number of Zunis hold positions in tribal government while others earn incomes from wage labor—for example, as construction workers or waitresses in Gallup. Relatively few are involved in livestock tending, and agricultural activities are limited to raising vegetables for food and blue and white corn for ceremonial purposes. The most popular source of income is silversmithing and the making of turquoise jewelry. Such work was originally done by men, but for some years now women have also been active in this craft. Zuni craftspeople are particularly well known for their "needlepoint" style, using settings of small hand-polished turquoise stones, and for inlay work, in which pieces of turquoise, shell, coral, and other stones are applied to a silver base. In addition to Zuni Pueblo, the principal town, the Zuni reside in several outlying farming villages and sheep camps.

The Acoma and the Laguna

To the present day the Acoma live in their pre-Columbian location about 60 miles west of Albuquerque. Their reservation, about 400 square miles in area, lies just south of Interstate 40 at an altitude ranging from 6,000 to 8,000 feet with an average precipitation of only 10 inches a year. There are three Acoma communities. Acomita and McCartys, two farming villages about 6 miles apart, began as farming and herding camps. The third, 10 miles to the south, is Acoma, the old pueblo on the mesa top that along with Old Oraibi on Third Mesa and Taos Pueblo claims to be the oldest continuously inhabited village north of Mexico. Perched about 400 feet above the surrounding area, Acoma is sometimes referred to by outsiders as Sky City. Today Acoma serves primarily as a ceremonial center and attracts visitors because of its spectacular location.

The Acoma people's first contact with Europeans was with a member of Coronado's expedition in 1540. They maintained relatively peaceful relations with the Spaniards until the end of the century. In 1599, when some of the villagers refused to become vassals of the Spanish Crown and attacked and killed a detachment of Spanish soldiers camped on Acoma mesa, Oñate ordered the village destroyed. Those who escaped the massacre eventually rebuilt and repopulated the village. Beginning in 1629, friendly relations developed between the villagers and the friar assigned to them. With the villagers' help, he was able to build a church at Acoma. But later in the century, efforts by the Spaniards to suppress native religious beliefs and practices caused such deterioration in relations with the Acoma that they joined the other Pueblo peoples in the Pueblo Revolt of 1680. In 1699 Acoma was among the last villages to resubmit to Spanish rule.

Throughout the following centuries the Acoma maintained peaceful—if at times somewhat tense—relations with the Spaniards, the Mexicans, and eventually the Americans. At times, though, disputes developed over land boundaries and other matters. One dispute, which happened to be with the neighboring Laguna, concerned a painting of Saint Joseph that had been given to the Acoma mission by King Charles II of Spain in 1629. The painting was believed to have miraculous powers, and the relative prosperity of the Acoma in the succeeding decades seemed to bear this out. After a time of drought and epidemic, the Laguna wanted to borrow the painting to benefit from its powers. The Acoma refused permission, but the painting was taken anyway. When some years later the Laguna refused to return it, the Acoma took their complaint to the U.S. judicial system. In 1857 the matter was finally settled by the U.S. Supreme Court—in favor of the Acoma.

Traditional culture among the Acoma has been quite strong, and their system of tribal government was little influenced by the Indian Reorganization Act of 1934. As in the other Western Pueblo societies, the Acoma social and ceremonial organization has been based on clans (19 of them reported in 1979). Descent follows the maternal line, and households have been matrilocal (married daughters bringing their husbands to live in their mother's house), although young people are now establishing independent households. The Acoma have always been agriculturalists. In the early years of the twentieth century they were able to increase production considerably, especially of sheep, horses, and wheat. Twenty years later, the main products were sheep, corn, and alfalfa. And by about 1940 plant production had diminished and the numbers of sheep and cattle expanded.

*   *   *

The reservation of the Laguna people borders the Acoma Reservation on the east and extends both north and south of Interstate 40. With an area of about 700 square miles, it is almost twice as large as the Acoma Reservation. The six major villages from north to south are Paguate, Encinal, Paraje, Seama, Old Laguna, and Mesita (the names given here are those found on maps; Laguna names for them are quite different). Old Laguna serves as the political center of the reservation. The language of the Laguna differs only slightly from the language of the Acoma. The two are considered to be dialects of Keres (the only language of the Keresan language family, mentioned earlier).

In comparison with most of the other pueblos of the Southwest, the Laguna communities are young. The founding of Old Laguna goes back to the very last years of the seventeenth century and is a result of the Pueblo Revolt. When the Spanish reoccupied Pueblo country in 1692, several pueblos rebelled against the reimposing of Spanish rule. Some of the rebels sought refuge in Zuni, others in Acoma. In 1697 those at Acoma, together with some disgruntled Acomas, moved down from the mesa and founded Laguna Pueblo about 14 miles to the northeast.

The culture of the Laguna is similar to that of the Acoma, but the Laguna became more pastoral, owning over 50,000 sheep by 1935. Later the number of sheep was drastically reduced as part of the U.S. government's program to protect the land from severe erosion caused by overgrazing. Shamans and religious societies were important to Laguna spiritual life. The religious societies were responsible for rituals concerning curing, fertility, ensuring the yearly succession of the seasons, and the reproduction of game animals and the successful hunting of these animals by the Laguna.

In the early 1950s mineral deposits were discovered on the reservation. Mining operations were soon employing several hundred Laguna residents. Other enterprises (federal, tribal, and private) provided employment for additional Lagunas. As a result, by the 1970s the Laguna may have been the most affluent Pueblo people.

*   *   *

To summarize, the Western Pueblo societies may differ from one another in the languages they speak and their culture and historical experience, but they share a number of cultural patterns. One of their major concerns is with the weather. All the Western Pueblos are agricultural people, and successful production of both crops and animals requires water, a scarce commodity in much of the Southwest. In social and ceremonial organization, the Western Pueblo peoples are characterized by clans with descent traced through the maternal line, a ban on marrying a person from the same clan, postmarital residence with the wife's family, the economic dominance of women (they own the houses and land), and katsina cults (katsinas are supernaturals believed able to bring rain and well-being to a community if ceremonially petitioned). As one moves east from the Zuni to the Acoma and Laguna, ceremonial life becomes less public but continues to be quite strong.

The Pueblo peoples are talented artists and craftspeople, producing wood carvings (kachinas), pottery, and silver and turquoise jewelry. The quality of their work is so high and their products so much desired that we have devoted a separate chapter, Chapter 5, to Southwestern arts and crafts.

Population figures for the various Pueblo peoples are not easy to come by, and the available figures may or may not include those individuals who choose to live off the reservation. As an example, colonies of Lagunas exist in Albuquerque; Holbrook,

Arizona; Los Angeles; and elsewhere, and their members may or may not be counted among the Laguna population. The figures below, which give population estimates for reservations and trust lands only, should be taken as approximate: Hopi (including the Tewa village of Hano)—9,000; Zuni—8,000; Acoma— more than 3,000; and Laguna—more than 4,000.

The Eastern Pueblos

The Eastern Pueblos are located on relatively small reservations on both sides of the Rio Grande, a few of them as far as 40 miles from its banks. Starting from the north, the reservation of the Taos people is located west and northeast (the famous old Taos Pueblo) of what has grown up as the town of Taos. Next are the Picuris, a short distance to the south. Farther southwest along the Rio Grande, north of Santa Fe, is a cluster of reservations belonging to the San Juan, Santa Clara, Pojoaque, San Ildefonso, Nambe, and Tesuque. Still farther southwest along the river, in another cluster of reservations, are the Jemez, Zia, Cochiti, Santo Domingo, Santa Ana, and San Felipe. Just north of Albuquerque is the reservation of the Sandia. And south of the city, lying on both sides of the Rio Grande, is the reservation of the Isleta. All these people speak languages belonging to one of two language families. The Cochiti, San Felipe, Santa Ana, Santo Domingo, and Zia speak dialects of Keres, and are therefore closely related to the Acoma and Laguna, who speak the other dialects of Keres. All the other Eastern Pueblo peoples speak Tanoan languages of the Kiowa-Tanoan language family; the Tanoan languages divide into three branches—Tewa, Tiwa, and Towa. (In addition to these sixteen Pueblo peoples, one more should be mentioned for the sake of completeness. It is the Tigua people, located within the southern boundary of El Paso, Texas. The Tigua have almost completely adapted to the larger society around them—their first language is Spanish, and their second English.)

General Background

In our overview of the history of the Western Pueblos, we pointed out that after Coronado's expedition to the American

Southwest in 1540–1542, much effort was expended for nearly three centuries in attempts to root out native religious beliefs and practices and replace them with Christianity. What we said then about the early history of the area applies in general terms to the Pueblo peoples of New Mexico. As for their traditional cultures, similarities predominate throughout the Southwest, but differences do exist and bear mentioning. Some of the Pueblos, especially the Tewa-speaking villagers of the northern cluster of reservations, have two basic tribal subdivisions that trace descent through the paternal line and whose members may marry each other. The subdivisions have frequently been associated with either summer or winter. Santa Clara Pueblo, for example, had Summer and Winter subdivision chiefs who alternated in appointing the various pueblo officials and held different ceremonial responsibilities, going back to ancient times.

The katsina cult is not so strong among the Eastern as among the Western Pueblos, from whom the Tanoan-speaking Pueblos may have borrowed it. In the locations farthest north, among the Taos and Picuris, the cult fades out entirely. The clowns who perform in ceremonies are considered sacred even though they are permitted to indulge in what would otherwise be unacceptable behavior. In the Hopi villages clowns appear with the katsina dancers during ceremonies held in the village plazas. Among the Eastern Pueblos they commonly belong to one of two clown societies associated with the summer or winter season or with kiva groups. Medicine societies have been important among the Keres-speaking Pueblos, even though membership in them has been small. The village chief and his assistants have invariably been medicine men.

Among the Pueblos, the contrast between sacred and secular matters is by tradition minimal. The elaborate ceremonial life of the Pueblos has always stressed communal involvement. The villages of the Western Pueblos have been governed essentially by officials regarded as divinely guided. Political control in the east has typically been in the hands of a chief *(cacique)* and a council. Except in the Hopi villages and Hano, the Roman Catholic Church has played a significant role for many years now, even though over the past 100 years or so Protestant missionaries have also been active. Even so, traditional religious practices continue to take place, many of them in the privacy of the kivas.

The nature and degree of the adjustment of the various Eastern Pueblo peoples to influences from the larger society around them vary from one pueblo to the next. Some have tended to remain culturally traditional—for example, the Santo Domingo and San Felipe peoples. Others have made significant adaptations to the larger society. The Santa Clarans make extensive use of their reservation for tourist recreational activities (tours, camping, hunting, and fishing), and during the summer, with the payment of an admission fee, tourists are welcome to witness their colorful traditional dances. For Santa Clarans, joining the cash economy has meant that the out-migration of their young people has been quite low.

Understandably, most of these formerly agricultural peoples have by now become dependent primarily on wage work in towns or on ranches, government employment, or some sort of federal assistance. Their need for cash has stimulated the production of various crafts (pottery, drums, jewelry, baskets, and leather items) to the benefit of tourists and others interested in their work. For example, among the Picuris, Cochiti, Isleta, Jemez, Zia, and Tesuque peoples, pottery making has become an important economic activity, and active craft cooperatives have been established in several pueblos. Potters in some of them have become so well known and their products so prized that their work is often purchased by both museums and discriminating collectors. In this connection, we should mention at least the Santa Clarans for their polished black pottery, some with incised and carved designs; the San Ildefonsans for their pottery with dull black paint on a polished black surface and also pieces decorated in several colors (polychrome—frequently black and red on a light background); and the Zians for their fine waterproof orange-on-white pottery. But the visitors will find many other interesting items to buy in Indian arts and crafts centers, trading posts, and souvenir shops in the larger cities and towns of New Mexico: two-headed cylindrical drums made by the Cochiti from hollowed-out sections of cottonwood trunks, stunning turquoise and shell necklaces made by the Santo Domingos, and accomplished tempera and watercolor paintings done by individual artists from several pueblos. (Again, see Chapter 5 for more about Southwestern arts and crafts.)

The approximate population figures for the individual pueblos and, in some cases, the associated trust lands are

200 to 350 people: Picuris, Pojoaque, Sandia, and Tesuque;
400 to 600 people: Nambe, San Ildefonso, Santa Ana;
700 to 1,000 people: Zia and Cochiti;
1,100 to 1,500 people: Taos, Santa Clara, and San Juan;
1,800 to 2,300 people: Jemez and San Felipe;
more than 2,800 people: Isleta and Santo Domingo.

*   *   *

To summarize, despite the several centuries of contact with the Spaniards, Mexicans, and Americans, some of the Pueblo peoples have managed to retain much of their traditional culture. Although changes in their cultures have been taking place for some time now, many features of their social and political institutions and their ceremonial organizations have persisted side by side with the political and ceremonial systems of Spanish or Spanish-Catholic origin. Today the question is to what extent the drastic economic changes that have accompanied the shift from agricultural subsistence to a cash economy may affect the unity of Pueblo communities. In many villages the strong element of conservatism characteristic of Pueblo cultures seems not to have been seriously undermined.

Native Americans in Modern Society

Most Americans tend to think of Native Americans in terms of the history of this continent—as people who tried bravely, against impossible odds, to hold on to the land that for thousands of years had been theirs and to ways of life that had proved harmonious with their natural surroundings. Their forced relocation onto reservations by the U.S. government during the nineteenth century deprived most Native Americans of the opportunity to live as much as possible as their ancestors had lived, and in many cases attempts to force upon them the dominant culture brought only chaos and confusion. The social and economic problems on many reservations today are the result.

Although these problems should not be minimized, there is another side to Native American life that we need to be more aware of. Many Native Americans have become successful professional people in the larger American society—linguists and anthropologists with doctorates from prestigious universities, senators, judges, attorneys, physicians, college professors, social workers, poets, writers, musicians, radio and television announcers, architects, and so on and on. Most of these people's hearts and minds continue to be rooted in the spiritual culture of their forebears, and it is from them and other less celebrated Native Americans that the rest of us can learn much to help us meet and solve some of the intractable problems facing modern society—lack of respect for the elderly, degradation of the environment, racism, and the lack of integration of spiritual concepts and values in so much of modern daily life—to name just a few.

4

▣ THE SOUTHWEST'S OTHER ▣ PEOPLES: THE ATHAPASKANS, YUMANS, AND SOUTHERN UTO-AZTECANS

The tribal ranges of the Pueblo peoples during early historical times formed a shallow U, with one of its ends in today's northeastern Arizona (the Hopi) and the other east of the Rio Grande in northern New Mexico (the Taos). The Pueblo country was surrounded by about a dozen other peoples who spoke, and still speak today, languages belonging to three different language families. Since membership in a particular language family indicates a close relationship reaching deep into prehistory, we will cover the non-Pueblo peoples according to the language families to which they belong.

The Navajo and several of the Apache tribes—the Western Apache, the Chiricahua, the Mescalero, and the Jicarilla—speak Athapaskan languages (or dialects). The speakers of languages belonging to the Yuman language family—frequently referred to as Yumans—include the Havasupai, Walapai, Yavapai, Mohave, Quechan, Maricopa, and Cocopa. And the Pima, the Papago (or Tohono O'odham, as they call themselves and prefer to be called), and the Yaqui speak languages of the Southern branch of the Uto-Aztecan language family.

41

The Athapaskans:
The Navajo and Apache

Navajo Prehistory and History

According to anthropologists, the ancestors of today's Navajos and the closely related Apaches came to the Southwest from western Canada, where other Athapaskan tribes, from whom the Navajo separated about a thousand years ago, still live. Whether the waves of Navajo groups came to the Southwest by way of the Great Plains east of the Rocky Mountains or more directly from their northern homeland, or perhaps took both routes, has never been firmly established, just as the time of their arrival in the Southwest can only be estimated. Some anthropologists believe that the Navajo (and the Apache) reached the Southwest during the thirteenth century, but the majority are of the opinion that it was probably a century or two later. At any rate, by about 1600 the Navajo were well established in the Four Corners area, for the most part in what is now New Mexico. The Spanish colonists referred to them as Apaches de Nabajó. The term *Nabajó* (that is, *Navajo*) probably came from a Tewa word referring to a valley with cultivated fields. The name that the Navajo themselves use is *Diné*, meaning "the people." By the time the Spaniards encountered the Navajo and Apache, they were considered two separate peoples.

Both tribes were originally hunters, fishers, and gatherers. They used dogs for pulling loads, made effective use of sinew-backed bows, produced coiled baskets, and decorated their skin clothing with porcupine quills. Spanish documents from the end of the sixteenth century and the first half of the seventeenth referred to the Navajo as semisedentary people who grew maize but who also moved about a great deal in pursuit of game. They traded with the Pueblos, who had settled in the area long before the Athapaskans came from the north, but at other times they raided various Pueblo towns.

By 1800 the area in which the Navajo lived extended into most of northeastern Arizona east of the Colorado River and on both sides of the Little Colorado. From there they penetrated into west-central New Mexico almost as far as the Rio Grande. Although their occasional raiding of Pueblo villages made the

Pueblos wary of them, there were periods when the two were allied. The Navajo took part in the Pueblo Revolt of 1680 against the many injustices the Pueblo peoples had suffered under the Spaniards, who were closing their kivas, prohibiting their traditional ceremonies, and otherwise trying to destroy native traditions in order to impose their own religion and culture. And as if this were not enough, every year the villagers were forced to give their oppressors a portion of their harvest, which was not plentiful to begin with. In desperation, the Pueblos united and with the help of the Navajo attacked Spanish garrisons and settlements, killing or driving out missionaries and burning churches in order to be free to practice their traditional ways. But twelve years later the Spaniards began their reconquest of the area, although from then on their rule was less harsh than before. The Pueblos who had led the revolt fled to the Apaches or the Hopi. A number of them joined the Navajo in the San Juan River basin, with cultural consequences for their hosts' religion (a more structured cosmology and more elaborate ritual performances) as well as material culture (such borrowings as woven cloth, painted pottery, sandals, and gourd dippers).

When the Spanish Southwest became a U.S. territory at the end of the U.S.-Mexican War in 1848, the Navajo began the most tragic period in their history. Their relations with the United States were marred by many acts of violence, the majority of them committed against the Navajo rather than by them. For example, after a meeting in 1849, American troops shot a Navajo leader in the back and also killed several of his companions. Twelve years later, without any provocation, a number of Navajo women and children collecting their rations were shot by soldiers. Some Navajo were held as slaves in New Mexico, a practice that continued even after the Civil War. Relations between the U.S. authorities and the Navajo resisting restrictions on their freedom soon became so tense that on June 15, 1863, the military commander of New Mexico ordered the removal of the Navajo to Fort Sumner, which was to serve as the "tribal reformatory." (Some students of history have suggested that the removal of the Navajo was promoted by those who were eager to develop a trail across the Navajo country to make possible the mining of its minerals.) The troops destroyed Navajo dwellings as well as their cornfields and fruit trees and captured or shot their horses and sheep. With no homes, no food, and no place to hide, the Navajo had little choice but to surrender. During 1863 alone, over 1,000 Navajos were killed, wounded, or captured. In February 1864, some 1,500 Navajos were taken to Fort Sumner, followed less than a month later by an even larger group. By March 1865 the number of Navajos interned at Fort Sumner was more than 9,000. Only a small minority of Navajos were able to avoid internment by escaping to nearly inaccessible locations such as the areas around Navajo Mountain and north of the San Juan River.

The first rays of hope appeared in late 1866, when the military commander of New Mexico was relieved of his duties. Four months later, control of the Navajo became the responsibility of the Bureau of Indian Affairs. Then on June 1, 1868, a treaty was concluded between the United States and the Navajo that permitted them to return to where they had lived before their internment. Two weeks later a ten-mile-long column of Navajos, escorted by four cavalry companies, finally left Fort Sumner. The tragic period that began with the Long Walk to Fort Sumner, during which many Navajos died, and the subsequent internment, which many of the older people did not survive, had lasted five long years.

The Navajo Reservation set up under the 1868 treaty covered about 3.5 million acres. On a map it appeared as a rectangle bisected by the present New Mexico–Arizona state line. Expanded several times in later years, mostly into Arizona, it now totals over 15 million acres, mainly in northeastern Arizona but also in southeastern Utah and northwestern New Mexico. For purposes of comparison, the Navajo Reservation is much larger than the state of Massachusetts. Navajo population has also grown considerably. Today the number of Navajos living both on and off the reservation has reached more than a quarter of a million.

Navajo Culture—In the Past and Today

Navajo society is divided into fifty to sixty matrilineal clans (that is, clans that trace descent through the mother's line). Individuals may never marry anyone belonging to either the mother's or father's clan or, traditionally, the paternal grandfather's or maternal grandfather's clan. Since kinship is determined by clan affiliation, each person has numerous relatives, all of whom are bound together by the solidarity of kinship bonds. The strongest bond exists between a mother and her children. The bond between wife and husband can be easily dissolved. The status of Navajo women is high. Residence after marriage is usually with the wife's people, women own the property, and the woven products made by women have become a good source of family income.

The Navajo may have learned some basic farming skills from the Native Americans with whom they were in contact as they made their way to the Southwest, but the major influence must have come from the Pueblos, who had made a remarkable adjustment to an arid environment and become efficient farmers. With the Spaniards came the introduction of horses, sheep, and goats. Possessing horses greatly increased the mobility of the Navajo, and raising sheep and goats provided a fairly dependable supply of food. After the internment of the Navajo at Fort Sumner in the 1860s, farming lost a great deal of its importance. During this century the tendency has been to also raise cattle. Cash income from the sale of calves is of advantage to the Navajo, who are slowly but inevitably being drawn into the cash economy of the larger society. But sheep provide the Navajo with the mainstay of their diet as well as with wool for making rugs and saddle blankets.

Unlike the Pueblo peoples, the Navajo do not live in villages. Their most common social organization is the residence group, consisting of several households. In addition to the members of the extended family, such a grouping usually includes a herd of sheep, the land-use area, and sometimes fields used for farming. Now that many younger Navajo live by wage work, the traditional rules of residence frequently do not apply.

In earlier times Navajo extended families used to cluster in local groups, each led by a headman, but for some years now Navajo communities tend to be organized around trading centers and schools across their vast reservation. Today, the Navajo tribal council has more than 100 local chapters. The chapter system brings people together to discuss local problems as well as problems affecting the entire tribe. The seat of Navajo tribal government is in Window Rock, Arizona (just west of the Arizona–New Mexico state line). Window Rock is an impressive

Two Navajo women and a child in front of a "modern" six-sided hogan in the 1940s. The earth-covered roof and thick walls help to keep the interior warm in the winter and cool in the summer. Courtesy of Verde Valley School. Photo by Milton Snow.

administrative center, combining modern facilities with architecture influenced by Navajo culture (for example, the council house is modeled after an eight-sided hogan, the traditional Navajo dwelling). This blending of aspects of American society with their own time-tested cultural values is characteristic of the Navajo. Another illustration are the Navajo community colleges at Tsaile, Arizona, and Shiprock, New Mexico. They are dedicated to the maintenance of Navajo cultural heritage within the complex and changing world of which the Navajo are now a part, and their curricula include strong programs of Navajo and Native American studies.

Among the aspects of traditional culture that have persisted to the present have been Navajo ceremonialism and worldview. The Navajo believe that the universe is an orderly system in which all the parts have their proper place. It is up to people to accommodate to nature, not try to master it. When for some reason order is disrupted, evil, danger, and especially illness are likely to come about. Navajo rituals are directed toward restoring the lost harmony that has resulted in a specific problem. In the case of disease, the exact cause must be established by a diviner so that the appropriate ritual can be arranged for. The specialist then asked to conduct the ceremonial is known as the singer, almost invariably an older man.

It is the singer who sees to it that the ceremonial proceedings are complete in every detail and performed without error. Such ceremonies include consecrating the hogan where the ritual is held, praying, chanting, creating elaborate sandpaintings, and other ritual activities. The singer must have an extraordinary memory. According to a well-known anthropologist who had many years of contact with the Navajo, a singer who is able to direct a nine-night chant must know "at least as much as a man who sets out to memorize the whole of a Wagnerian opera: orchestral score, every vocal part, all the details of the settings, stage business, and each requirement of costume." And some singers know several long chants.

Do curing rites work? To believers, a ritual invariably gives such a powerful psychological boost that improvement in the patient's condition frequently follows. However, as we mentioned earlier, the Navajo are practical people who readily draw on what other cultures can contribute to their well-being. Many make use of the modern medical facilities available to them on or near the reservation, but often in conjunction with their native rites and medicine. Such people take the best from both worlds.

Navajo women are widely known for their weaving, men for their silver work. Many Navajos are such accomplished artists, weavers, and silversmiths that we have devoted several pages to their work in Chapter 5.

The Navajo-Hopi Land Dispute

Visitors to the Southwest who are interested in the relations among the various Native American peoples of the region are likely to hear mention of the land dispute between the Navajo and the Hopi. We will attempt to give a very brief account of a longtime dispute that has become more and more complicated.

During the eighteenth and nineteenth centuries, the Navajo, with their flocks of sheep, began to make use of lands closer and closer to the Hopi villages. According to a delegation of Hopi chiefs to Zuni requesting assistance with the problem in 1819, a few Navajos had settled only a few miles (two leagues) from First Mesa. To protect the Hopi from intrusions by both Navajos and whites, in 1882 the U.S. government set aside a rectangular area about 70 miles by 55 miles for the use and occupancy of the Hopi "and such other Indians [note the ambiguity] as the Secretary of the Interior may see fit to settle thereon." This area has come to be referred to as the 1882 Executive Order Area (EOA). Although the Hopi were living in their villages on the three mesas, they depended on the surrounding land, which they treasured as their homeland and where they grazed their cattle, planted their cornfields, and gathered wood.

Meanwhile the Navajo population was continuing to increase, and as a result occupied more and more of what the Hopi considered to be their territory, the boundaries of which were not marked. In 1958, feeling threatened by continued encroachment after many years of complaints and vain attempts to resolve the land disputes, the Hopi filed a suit against the Navajo. Four years later an Arizona court decided that the Hopi would have exclusive rights to one particular part of the EOA, termed District 6, and the Hopi and Navajo tribes "joint, undivided and equal rights and interests" to the rest of the EOA, some 1,800,000 acres. This large area has subsequently been referred to as the Joint Use Area (JUA). When the two tribes were unable to come to an agreement as to how to share the surface rights to the JUA, Congress in 1974 enacted the Navajo-Hopi Indian Land Settlement Act, which divided the JUA equally between the Hopi and the Navajo. Subsequently, the U.S. government acquired about 365,000 acres in Arizona adjacent to the reservation for Navajo relocation. About 2,650 Navajo families were to be relocated from the Hopi half, as were the 24 Hopi families who were living in the Navajo half. But relocating families from areas in which they have lived for many years (several generations in some cases) is a difficult matter. In 1988, fourteen years after the settlement act of 1974, more than 1,200 Navajo and 10 Hopi families were still to be relocated. This is why the 1974 settlement act was amended in 1988, the most important provision being the establishment of the Navajo Rehabilitation Trust Fund. But the Navajo tribal government continued to protest relocation, urging instead land exchanges with their neighbors—a position that was not acceptable to the Hopi.

In 1992 the Circuit Court Of Appeals appointed a mediator to help settle the dispute once and for all. Navajo Nation officials were willing to seriously consider ten Hopi preconditions for mediation, and the president of the Navajo Nation acknowledged the rights of the Hopi to the land partitioned to them as well as the willingness of the Hopi tribe to offer seventy-five-year leases, with certain limitations, to the remaining Navajo families residing on Hopi land. But such an arrangement was unacceptable to the Navajos concerned. They feared the possibility of lease cancellation for some cause during the seventy-five-year period and also the likelihood of losing their home territory altogether at the end of that period. Mediation continued during 1993 and 1994, with new proposals submitted by both the Navajo Nation and the Hopi tribe. Perhaps the resolution of this long dispute may at last be in sight. As of 1995 about 700 Navajo families were still to be relocated.

We have not taken sides in this short note on the land dispute because we have great respect for both the Navajo and the Hopi. On the one hand, the Navajo Reservation population, more than twenty times larger than the Hopi population, has been growing rapidly, and families that have sizable herds of sheep in an arid or semiarid environment need large areas for grazing. On the other hand, the Hopi are eager to hold on to what they consider their ancient homeland and to protect their fields from sheep, who in a few hours can destroy the results of long and careful cultivation.

The Apache

Soon after reaching the Southwest, probably around the fifteenth century, the Apachean population broke up into several independent groups that eventually developed separate dialects. Besides the Navajo, there came to be five main Apachean-speaking tribes—the Chiricahua, Jicarilla, Lipan, Mescalero, and Western Apache. (The Kiowa Apache, who now live in Oklahoma, have been culturally one of the Southern Great Plains peoples for nearly five centuries.) When Europeans first encountered them, the Apache people roamed over what today is eastern Arizona, New Mexico, adjoining parts of Mexico, western Oklahoma and Texas, southeastern Colorado, and western Kansas. Those in the eastern part of this large area—the Lipan, Mescalero, and Jicarilla—were on the edges of the Great Plains and not surprisingly were greatly influenced by the cultures of the Plains Indians. Like them, they became expert horsemen, lived in tepees, and hunted buffalo. Those Apache farthest to the west—the Chiricahua and the Western Apache—continued to hunt and gather. But they also learned from the Pueblos how to engage in agriculture and were able to supplement their diet by growing corn and melons, and later pumpkins, squash, and beans.

The Apache were brave fighters and their raids were feared by the Pueblo peoples as well as by the Spaniards and Anglo settlers. Their assertive behavior against those they saw as interlopers in areas traditionally belonging to Apaches continued even after New Mexico was annexed to the United States in 1846. They were not willing to be permanently settled, and led by such famous chiefs as Cochise (1812?–1874) and Geronimo (1829–1909), both Chiricahuas, they engaged the U.S. military forces in conflict for many years.

Although Cochise regarded Mexicans as enemies because of their severe reprisals against his people, he was willing to cooperate somewhat with the Americans. In 1858, for example, he agreed to let mail coaches pass through Chiricahua territory undisturbed. But before long, matters took a turn for the worse. In late January 1861, a young ambitious cavalry lieutenant requested a meeting with Cochise. When the chief, accompanied by several relatives and subchiefs, entered the lieutenant's tent, he was accused of having kidnapped a young boy. Cochise knew nothing about the boy but offered his help in finding him. Disregarding this offer of cooperation, the lieutenant gave an order to seize the Apaches and hold them hostage. Cochise managed to escape, but among the victims of the incident was Cochise's brother, who with others was later hanged from a scrub oak tree. War was on, with Cochise determined to fight the intrusion of settlers into Apache country. Massacres involving indiscriminate killing took place on both sides. Private citizens organized "Indian-hunting parties," and on one occasion a group of Apaches invited to participate in a peace conference was said to have been fed poisoned food. When in 1872 a Chiricahua Reservation in the southeast corner of Arizona Territory was temporarily established, Cochise finally gave himself up, and there he died in 1874.

After Cochise's death, Geronimo assumed leadership of the Chiricahua. Determined to keep his people free from confinement at another reservation, he and his followers were at constant odds with the U.S. authorities. On several occasions he was arrested and taken to San Carlos Reservation, but he always managed to escape, sometimes into northern Mexico. Finally on September 3, 1886, he was the last Native American leader to surrender to U.S. authorities, in Skeleton Canyon, Arizona, when he and a handful of warriors were outnumbered by 5,000 troops and 500 Indian scouts. First exiled to a prison camp in Florida and then later moved to another in Alabama, Geronimo died in 1909 at Fort Sill, Indian Territory (today's Oklahoma), never having been granted his earnest wish to return to, or at least revisit, his beloved Apache country in southeastern Arizona.

The Western Apache

To acquaint the reader with traditional Apache culture, we describe here the Western Apache as typical of that way of life. The Western Apache include all the Apache groups (except the Chiricahua and several small bands) who lived during historic times in what today is Arizona. From southeast to northwest, the Western Apache divisions were the San Carlos Apache, White Mountain Apache, Cibecue Apache, and the Southern and Northern Tonto Apache.

Originally hunters and gatherers who lived in hide-covered dwellings and moved periodically from place to place, during the seventeenth and eighteenth centuries the Western Apache learned from their Pueblo neighbors to cultivate vegetable crops, although crops were never a major part of their subsistence. After the Spaniards introduced the horse into the Southwest and it became a part of Native American life, the Western Apache became not only very active traders but also raiders all the way from the Hopi mesas in the north to what would now be south of the U.S. border. During the winter months small groups of men (a dozen or so) would surprise both Spanish and Native American settlements during the early morning hours, making off with their livestock, which were what the Apache were after.

Each Western Apache division consisted of several bands, and each band of several local groups—extended families residing with the wife's kin group. Clans reckoned through the mother's side cut across these divisions. As with many other Native American groups, members of the same clan could not marry each other. It was traditional for men to practice strict mother-in-law avoidance. If crossing paths with his mother-in-law was unavoidable for a man, he did his best not to look at her. Rarely did a man take more than one wife, but if he did, the women were likely to be sisters. The most prominent leaders of the Western Apache, the chiefs of the local groups, were respected not only for their skills in hunting and raiding but also for their generosity, their industriousness, and their eloquence.

Like the Navajo, many of the Western Apache have a rich and intricate mythology telling of the creation of the earth and of the first humans' emergence from beneath the earth's surface. One of their favorite mythical figures has always been Coyote. On the one hand, he was supposed to have taught the Apache how to plant corn, weave baskets, and engage in other useful cultural activities, but on the other, he was a mischievous character who frequently deserved punishment—in other words, he exhibited very human characteristics.

Again like the Navajo, the Apache had a fear of the dead and of the ghosts of the deceased. This is why they buried dead relatives with great dispatch and burned their dwellings and possessions. The family then moved to another location, and it was forbidden to utter the name of a deceased relative for at least fifteen years.

It was believed that either supernatural power could simply come to individuals or individuals could search for it. Those it came to were considered particularly worthy persons, and among them were the shamans (medicine men). They were the ones who instructed others in the performance of elaborate ceremonials. The rituals required the mastery of a great many chants using specialized language that differed from everyday Apache. The ceremonies were performed to cure people of illness, which was thought to result from the violation of the various taboos of the Apache culture.

The Contemporary Situation

Today, the Apache of the Southwest live on reservations, the earliest of which were established during the 1870s. In Arizona, the two large Apache reservations are the San Carlos Reservation and, adjoining it to the north, Fort Apache Reservation. Together these two reservations cover about 3.5 million acres 100 miles or so east of Phoenix. There are also three small Apache reservations in Arizona—Fort McDowell Reservation on the northeast edge of metropolitan Phoenix; Tonto Apache Reservation near the town of Payson, some 100 miles northeast of Phoenix; and Camp Verde Reservation at Camp Verde, about 90 miles north of Phoenix.

In New Mexico, there are two Apache reservations: the Jicarilla Apache Reservation northeast of Santa Fe, with its northern boundary coinciding with the New Mexico–Colorado state line, and the Mescalero Apache Reservation (Mescaleros, Chiricahuas, and Lipans) about 190 miles southeast of Albuquerque. Together, these two reservations cover well over 1 million acres. The Apache who live on the reservations in New Mexico and Arizona numbered about 25,000 in 1995.

During their 500 or so years in the Southwest, the Apache have made a number of cultural adaptations. Cattle ranching and the wage economy of the American society have been their most recent sources of income. They have also been able to increase land holdings—in 1970 the Jicarilla, for example, were awarded more than 9 million acres in the northeastern part of the Southwest to compensate them for the damages suffered by the U.S. government's expropriation of an even larger area in 1883.

The Yumans

Although for at least 1,000 years the prehistoric and historic home of the Yuman-speaking peoples has been mainly a desert area, the people became efficient farmers along the Colorado and Gila Rivers. Both rivers overflowed every year, providing moisture and depositing a layer of silt on land adjacent to them. Yuman-speaking peoples are made up of Upland Yumans in northwest and north-central Arizona: the Havasupai, Walapai, and Yavapai; and the River Yumans along the lower Colorado and Gila: the Mohave, Maricopa, Quechan, and Cocopa.

The Upland Yumans—the Havasupai, Walapai, and Yavapai—are closely related. The dialects of the Havasupai and the Walapai are nearly identical; the subdialects of the Yavapai, however, are differentiated not only from Havasupai and Walapai but also from each other. All these dialects are considered to be varieties of one language (referred to as Upland Yuman or Northern Pai).

The Havasupai

During the early 1800s the territory of the Havasupai extended south from the Grand Canyon section of the Colorado River about 70 miles, and about 90 miles from east to west at its widest point. But in the latter half of the century cattle ranchers and copper prospectors had encroached upon the area to such a degree that in 1880 a reservation had to be established for the Havasupai. Competition for land kept increasing not only from cattlemen but also from the Navajo to the east and the Walapai to the west, with the result that the natural resources of the surrounding areas became so depleted that by the 1950s the Havasupai could depend on only 518 acres of their reservation. The pressures from other populations were finally relieved after Congress passed a bill in 1974 establishing for the Havasupai a reservation of more than 180,000 acres and granting them an additional 93,000 acres in Grand Canyon National Park south of the Colorado River for their permanent use. Today the Havasupai Reservation is probably the most isolated Native American reservation in the United States.

The traditional subsistence of the Havasupai consisted of farming along the floor of Havasu Creek Canyon—an offshoot of Grand Canyon—during the summer and hunting and gathering on the Coconino Plateau during the winter. In October families would move to their camps on the forested plateau, where they lived on deer, mountain sheep, antelope, rabbit, piñon nuts, and various other wild plant foods. Then in early spring they moved to their summer homes in the canyon, where they repaired their dwellings and prepared their fields for planting. Originally raising corn, beans, and squash, they later added peaches, apricots, sunflowers, and figs—crops that grew well on the canyon floor, about 2,000 feet lower than their winter camps on the Coconino Plateau.

The Havasupai were active traders, trading their baskets, buckskins, and foodstuffs with other Native American groups for jewelry, pottery, woven blankets, and horses. Raising horses became an important activity toward the end of the nineteenth century.

The basic unit of Havasupai society was the family, consisting of the parents and their children, and sometimes additional relatives. Each family was an independent economic unit. After a temporary residence with the wife's parents, a young couple went to live with the husband's parents. The Havasupai had no other social divisions based on kinship or rank. Individuals recognized as tribal chiefs had no power to make decisions, but their advice was valued on all sorts of matters, especially if the chief was a person of notable achievement and wide experience.

The most important ceremony of the Havasupai was the harvest-time round dance held in the fall. This celebration, which lasted two or three days, was both a religious and a social occasion, with members of neighboring tribes invited to participate. Today this celebration has evolved into the Havasupai annual Peach Festival, which is usually held during the Labor Day weekend. Havasupai religious beliefs for the most part have been associated with the soul, dreams, and the curing of sickness. Ill health was thought to be caused by harmful dreams, sorcery, ghosts, or other supernatural forces, and great importance has been given to the shamans, who were believed to possess special powers to cure the sick and control events.

In recent years the Havasupai, like other Native Americans of the Southwest, have made significant cultural and economic adjustments. Their cash economy depends to a large measure on wage employment and the tourist trade. Because the descent (and later ascent) by 8-mile trail from Hualapai Hilltop to Supai, the reservation center on Havasu Creek, involves a difference of 2,000 feet in altitude (from 5,200 to 3,200 feet above sea level), some tourists prefer to make the trip on horseback. This service is supplied by the Havasupai. Other Havasupais are employed at Grand Canyon Village on the canyon's South Rim, which several million people visit each year. As of 1995 the number of Havasupai enrolled as tribal members was just over 600.

*   *   *

A note to hikers: One and a half miles downstream from Supai in Havasu Canyon are the 75-foot-high Navajo Falls and farther downstream Havasu Falls, about 100 feet high. The trail leads next to Mooney Falls (nearly 200 feet high, much higher than Niagara Falls) and then to Beaver Falls. At this point the junction of Havasu Creek with the Colorado River is only about 4 miles farther downstream. Use of the trail can be arranged at Supai.

To reach Hualapai Hilltop, the trailhead to Supai, take Arizona State Road 66 northwest from I-40 at Seligman for 28 miles, and then Indian Service Road 18 for 63 miles. This road is paved all the way to Hualapai Hilltop, but there are no services after the turnoff from SR 66. Havasu Campground is available about 11 miles from Hualapai Hilltop, and accommodations for a limited number of visitors are provided at Supai. Reservations should be made well in advance for either of these through Havasupai Tourist Enterprise at Supai, AZ 86435. There is a charge for entering the reservation as well as for camping.

The Walapai

During the nineteenth century the dozen or so divisions of the Walapai tribe (also spelled Hualapai) occupied an area in today's northwestern Arizona north of Flagstaff and Bill Williams River up to the Colorado River in the north and the Little Colorado in the east. They were primarily hunters and gatherers, depending on rabbits, birds, deer, bighorn sheep, and pronghorn antelope as well as cacti, piñon nuts, juniper berries, and other wild plant food. For example, the Walapai baked the stalks of mescal, a small cactus with rounded stems, in earth ovens and then ate the inner core and crushed the outer layers into a pulp, which they dried and stored. Until their traditional culture was disrupted by Anglo settlers, some Walapais who lived along rivers and streams were also efficient agricultural- ists, using diversion dams to irrigate gardens in which they grew beans, squash, maize, watermelon, and wheat.

Walapai camps were made up of several families; a headman coordinated the activities of the group and offered advice. Sev- eral neighboring camps formed a band, and several bands a sub- tribe. Despite the extensive area that the Walapai considered their home territory, their total population around 1860 proba- bly did not exceed 1,000. Active traders, the Walapai not only bartered with the neighboring Havasupai and Mohave, with whom they traded meat and skins for such cultivated foods as corn, pumpkins, and beans, but they even became involved in an exchange system between the Native Americans of the Pacific coast and the Pueblos. Among trade items were the highly val- ued baskets woven by the Walapai women. The religious beliefs of the Walapai were similar to those held by the Havasupai, with shamans playing an important role. Walapai mourning cer- emonies for the dead were elaborate.

The first contact of the Walapai with Europeans took place toward the end of the 1700s when the Walapai were visited by a Spanish Franciscan missionary. Anglos did not enter the tribal territory until the 1850s. Friction began to develop a decade later in the vicinity of Prescott when the Walapai felt threatened by gold prospectors. Several serious engagements with U.S. troops occurred during the latter half of the 1860s, and the Walapai were forced to surrender to the better-armed Anglo sol- diers. As a consequence, the Walapai were interned, and in 1874 they were removed south to the Colorado River Reservation near La Paz. But conditions there were so unsatisfactory that the Walapai fled. Barely a year later, they were rounded up and taken back to the reservation, but once again they found life there unbearable and returned to what they considered their home territory farther to the north. A 900,000-acre reservation was then established for them south of the Colorado River, ad- jacent to the Havasupai Reservation to the east. Still the Wala- pai suffered from the encroachment of cattle ranchers, and when they tried to defend their land they were treated as a nuisance by the Anglos. At one point they were so poverty-stricken that food rations had to be issued to them to help them survive. No wonder that when the Ghost Dance revival occurred and this religious movement was introduced to the Walapai by Southern Paiutes in 1889, the Walapai eagerly accepted it. They hoped that the constant performance of the Ghost Dance rituals, as its prophet Wovoka preached, would somehow turn back the tide of Anglos and restore the traditional ways of life. (The first wave of the Ghost Dance had occurred twenty years earlier and involved especially Native Americans of California.)

Today, most of the Walapai, whose enrolled members number close to 2,000, live in the only reservation town, Peach Springs, which is the tribal headquarters, as well as off the reservation at Big Sandy, southeast of Kingman, and in several railroad communities between Kingman and Seligman. The main sources of income for the Walapai are cattle ranching, harvesting lumber, and fees for operating rafting trips through the lower Grand Canyon.

The Yavapai

Until the 1860s, when the Anglos began encroaching into their home territory, the Yavapai roamed in what today is central and west-central Arizona from the San Francisco Peaks (near Flagstaff) to the Pinal Mountains (south of Globe) in the east, and from the Colorado River where Lake Havasu City is today to Martinez Lake (north of Yuma) in the west.

Archaeologists have not been able to agree fully on the prehistory of the Yavapai people. Some have suggested that the Hakataya tradition was probably ancestral to the Yavapai culture, others have assumed descent from southern Sinagua peoples, and still others have proposed a Yuman migration from the west after A.D. 1100. Historical information from the eighteenth and nineteenth centuries indicates that the Yavapai were fierce fighters and were feared by many of their Native American neighbors. For a long time they were closely associated with the Apache and as a result were frequently confused with them. Under constant pressure from the Anglos, who began invading their homeland in the early 1860s, the Yavapai agreed in 1865 to share the Colorado River Reservation with several other tribes. But the area was not large enough to yield sufficient crops, and before long the Yavapai left.

The 1870s were very difficult years for the Yavapai people. Of the several massacres of Yavapais carried out by U.S. troops, the most horrendous was the slaughter late in 1872 of a sizable band of Yavapai men, women, and children who had sought refuge in a Salt River Canyon cave, afterward known as Skeleton Cave. By 1873 the majority of the Yavapai had been forced onto the newly created Rio Verde Reservation located along the Verde River near Camp Verde. Conditions on the new reservation were hard, but the Yavapai, using only their own simple tools, were able to develop an irrigation system that soon allowed them to produce good harvests. Realizing that the Yavapai at Rio Verde were becoming self-sufficient, contractors with the U.S. government who were the suppliers for reservations put pressure on the government to revoke the Rio Verde Reservation and, in spite of the objections of the commanding general, to move the Yavapai to the Apache Reservation at San Carlos.

In 1875, the Yavapai were relocated to San Carlos Apache Reservation. During the midwinter march there from the Rio Verde Reservation, more than 100 Yavapais died as a result of the insufficient supplies provided them for the 180 miles of rough terrain that had to be traversed on foot (the soldiers accompanying them rode ponies). Not until the 1880s and 1890s were the Yavapai permitted to return to their original lands. Some chose to remain at San Carlos and intermarried with the Apaches living there.

Traditionally the Yavapai were hunters and gatherers, supplementing their diet of small animals, deer, and native wild plants with modest crops of corn, beans, and squash planted along stream bottomlands. The social organization of the Yavapai was similar to that of the Havasupai and Walapai, with the family as the basic unit for making decisions and producing food. Each local group recognized a leader who advised members not only on matters of practical consequence but also on how to "live right." At times of war expeditions, local groups had their own war chiefs—experienced warriors who had proved themselves in the past.

Yavapai women were widely known for their baskets made to serve various utilitarian purposes such as gathering foodstuffs, carrying burdens, winnowing, and carrying and storing water. Baskets for water were tightly woven and then coated with pitch. Yavapai coiled baskets were often traded with the Navajo and other neighboring peoples. These baskets have been a popular item with tourists, but today not many Yavapai women still have the skills required to practice the traditional art of Yavapai basket weaving.

According to Yavapai mythology, the world was destroyed three times in the past and will be destroyed once more at some future time. Both humans and animals are believed to have originally ascended to the earth's surface on the first maize plant through an opening in what has become known as Montezuma Well, a large sinkhole located near Camp Verde and a very sacred place for the Yavapai. The Yavapai pray for good health, and their medicine people have great prestige. Other than Montezuma Well, the most sacred places of the Yavapai are in the beautiful canyons of the red rock country near Sedona.

Today, most of the Yavapai people live on several reservations in Arizona: the Yavapai-Prescott Reservation just north of Prescott (1,400 acres), Fort McDowell Reservation just northeast of Phoenix (25,000 acres), and Camp Verde Reservation near Camp Verde, about 90 miles north of Phoenix. The 653 acres of the Camp Verde Reservation are divided among areas near Camp Verde, Middle Verde, and other nearby locations. The total number of Yavapais is not easy to determine because of intermarriage with members of other tribes, especially the Apaches, but it may now exceed 1,000. For most of them farming is no longer a viable source of subsistence. Many now are wageworkers in a reservation motel, a casino, and various small-scale enterprises. Others earn money off the reservation.

The Mohave, Quechan, Cocopa, and Maricopa (the River Yumans)

The original locations of the River Yumans were along the lower Colorado River, the border between Arizona and California, but several centuries ago the Maricopa moved to southwestern Arizona and made their home along the Gila River. Today, most members of these tribes reside on reservations. The

Mohave are located mainly on the 23,000-acre Fort Mohave Reservation in Arizona, which crosses the Nevada and California borders, with some living with other Native Americans on the Colorado River Reservation. The Maricopa occupy the Salt River Reservation just east of Phoenix and the Gila River Reservation south of Phoenix, sharing the areas with the Pima. The Quechan (sometimes referred to as the Yuma) were assigned land on the Fort Yuma Reservation near the confluence of the Colorado and Gila Rivers just north of Yuma. And the Cocopa have their own small reservation in the far southwest corner of the state, although most of the Cocopa now live just south of the border in Mexico. When first encountered by the Spaniards during the sixteenth and seventeenth centuries, all four peoples lived in approximately the same locations as they do today.

None of these peoples had true villages. Their settlements, scattered along the river on low bluffs or valley slopes to avoid flooding, consisted of a local group made up of an extended family or several related families. Except for the coldest parts of the year, when they used more permanent dwellings, they preferred to live in shades *(ramadas),* which protected them from the sun but otherwise were open. Farming along river bottomlands, they grew maize, beans, melons, squash, and other crops. These were supplemented with wild plants, some of the small game (mostly rabbits) that lived in the desert environment, and especially fish from the river. Although items of their material cultures were simple and utilitarian, these peoples were not without skills—for example, pottery making was common among the Cocopa and Quechan, the making of fishing equipment among the Mohave, and cotton weaving among the Maricopa.

Although related by virtue of a common ancestry, the River Yumans were known to fight one another from time to time. In such situations the Mohave and Quechan were usually allied. The battles had a ritual quality to them, with both individual and tribal prestige, rather than material gain, the goal.

Ceremonial practices in the Southwest have been rich and among many Pueblo peoples are still thriving. Among the River Yumans, the emphasis has been on curing and on dream experiences rather than on public ceremonialism. Among the Mohave, for example, it was those few with "great dreams" who were most likely to become tribal leaders—chiefs, exceptional braves, and shamans. In general, the shamans among these people were believed to be able not only to cure sickness but also to cause it—to bewitch people. At times, if it was thought that they had used their power for evil purposes, they could find their lives in danger, and in fact there were instances when shamans were killed. The most important ceremonies among the River Yumans had to do with death. Relatives and friends assembled to sing and wail when someone was about to die. Remains were cremated, with speeches made and songs sung to remind the mourners of the person's virtues. Traditionally, the property of the deceased was destroyed, occasionally with mourners adding some of their own belongings to the flames. The soul of the deceased was believed to depart to the spirit land, though not to live forever, and once the ashes were covered with earth, the name of the person was never again mentioned. An annual mourning ceremony was considered so important that most River Yumans made every attempt to participate.

Today, the River Yumans have adapted to the larger society around them, generally making their livelihood from wage work and, in some instances, from the leasing of some of their land. The small amount of farming that is currently carried on makes use of both modern equipment and irrigation. It is not easy to determine the total membership of these four tribes—the figure of around 12,000 is only an estimate.

*   *   *

An additional note: In prehistoric times a small population of some 600 or 700 Native Americans lived a nomadic life in the eastern half of the Mohave Desert. Since they spoke a dialect of a Uto-Aztecan language, they were not related to the River Yumans, but eventually they came to be known by their Yuman name, Chemehuevi. During the early 1800s the Mohave allowed these people to farm along the Colorado River. As a result the Chemehuevi became strongly influenced by the Mohave and other neighboring Yumans, not only in their material culture but in their religion as well. Today the Chemehuevi live on the Colorado River Reservation together with other Native Americans.

Southern Uto-Aztecans

The Pima and the Tohono O'odham (Papago)— A Brief History

Most of the people in northwestern New Spain at the beginning of the seventeenth century lived in scattered settlements and raised crops. Among them were Piman-speaking people who stayed in mountain villages in the winter but descended to valley settlements during the growing season to plant and harvest corn, squash, and beans. The area they occupied extended from the northern shores of the Gulf of California in what is now Mexico through today's southwestern, central, and southeastern Arizona.

Those who lived in the northern half of this area were referred to by the Spaniards as Upper Pimans. The living descendants of these people are the Pima and the Papago, or the Tohono O'odham, as the Papago now prefer to be called. Today, the Pima live on the Ak-Chin, Gila River, and Salt River Reservations and the neighboring urban areas of south-central Arizona, as well as in the mountains south of the border. The Tohono O'odham can be found on the Papago (Tohono O'odham), Ak-Chin, Gila Bend, and San Xavier Reservations, as well as south of the border in northern Sonora and as far away as Los Angeles and San Jose in California.

Continuous contact of Upper Pimans with Europeans developed toward the end of the seventeenth century when the Jesuits began establishing numerous missions in the area. Although Upper Pimans resented and had occasionally rebelled against the Spaniards, some of them were enlisted by the missionaries to help stop the Apache who were repeatedly pressing against the eastern boundaries of the Upper Piman area. During the late 1760s, Franciscan friars replaced the Jesuits, who were expelled from New Spain by edict of the Spanish king. Under the Franciscans the influence of the missions continued. Not only the traditional beliefs but also the material culture of the Upper Pimans were affected. Horses, cattle, and wheat, introduced by the Spaniards, came to play more and more important roles in their economy.

After Mexico became independent in 1821, many Mexican farmers, ranchers, and miners began migrating north and encroaching on some of the Upper Pimans to such an extent that for three years a state of war existed between the newcomers and the Native Americans. The end result, of course, was that the Pimans were forced to capitulate. A new wave of immigrants—especially Anglo-American miners—began competing for Piman homeland once the northernmost part of New Spain became part of the United States at the end of the Mexican War in 1848. Soon after the southern boundary of the United States became fixed, differentiation began to be made among the Piman speakers. Those who lived along the Gila River were referred to as Pima, those who lived farther south and west as Papago (now Tohono O'odham). The languages of the two are so closely related that they are considered dialects of one language.

To protect the Pima and Papago from continuing loss of homeland, in 1857 the U.S. government extended its Indian policy to both groups and began to grant them reservations. To begin with, in 1859 a reservation was set aside for the Pima and Maricopa (the Gila River Reservation).

Traditional Cultures of the Pima and Tohono O'odham

It is possible that the Pima and the Tohono O'odham are the descendants of the Hohokam (their culture is briefly discussed in Chapter 2). Because the amount of annual precipitation over the large area where these two peoples lived varies from practically none to about 15 inches, they had to adapt to differing environmental conditions. Both groups depended at least partly on growing crops (primarily maize, beans, and squash). For the Pima, who called themselves the River People and who were aided in their intensive farming by communal irrigation projects, agriculture provided over half their subsistence needs. For the Tohono O'odham, the Desert People, who lived in an area with no permanent streams, the comparable figure was only about one-fourth. Both peoples had to rely to some extent on wild plants, a variety of animals ranging from deer to lizards, such insects as grasshoppers, and in the case of the Pima, also on whatever fish they could catch in the river.

The permanence of the settlements of these peoples depended on the reliability of the local water supply. Pima dwellings, along streams, irrigation canals, or near wells, ranged from simple brush enclosures to round or oval houses, with flat roofs supported by beams. By contrast, those Papago groups who frequently had to move from place to place built only light temporary structures. Although there was a tendency for a young couple to reside in the household of the husband's father, a residence might also be established with the help of the husband's maternal relatives or relatives of the wife.

Each local group had a headman whose opinions were listened to but who had no power to enforce decisions. Because the Pima had fairly permanent villages, their political organization was stronger than that of the Papago. For example, the village headmen elected a tribal chief. In each community a shaman, deriving his power from his dreams, conducted various ceremonies, most of which had to do with foretelling the future, using magic for the benefit of the members of his group, or diagnosing and removing the causes of illness. Subsequent ministrations to patients were then entrusted to healers.

In midsummer the Tohono O'odham observed an important ceremony during which wine made from the fruit of the saguaro cactus was drunk in large quantities. It was believed that just as the men became saturated with the wine, so their fields would be soaked with rainwater and their crops flourish.

Contemporary Situation

Today, the Upper Pimans have adapted to the American society that surrounds them, and the claim has been made by an outside observer that the Gila Pima may be—for better or for worse—the most culturally assimilated Native Americans in the Southwest. Their literacy rate is high, with education on the reservations provided by public, Bureau of Indian Affairs, and church schools. Many young people go on to college. Employment is in part agricultural (on tribal farms), but people also work in tribal government and in several industrial parks on the reservations. Leasing land to Anglo farmers and mining companies brings additional income.

Pima women have been known for their expertly woven and beautifully decorated baskets, but today only a few devote their time to basket making. In contrast, the Tohono O'odham produce many baskets of high quality that are sold every year at fairs and rodeos and in trading posts and museum shops.

The size of the Pima and Tohono O'odham populations can only be estimated. Including those who live on the various reservations, in Arizona cities and towns, and outside the state, the Pima number 12,000 or more, and the Tohono O'odham between 16,000 and 20,000.

The Yaqui

The home of the Yaqui was originally a sizable area on both sides of the Yaqui River, which empties into the Gulf of California west of Ciudad Obregón in the Mexican state of Sonora. At the beginning of the nineteenth century the Yaqui claimed a territory of about 6,000 square miles in southern Sonora. For most of that century they were able to resist Mexican settlement of their fertile land, but toward the end of it their tribal lands were occupied by Mexican federal troops. Even then the Yaqui refused to accept Mexican authority, and as a consequence about 5,000 of them were sold as slaves, at 60 pesos per person, to plantation operators in Yucatan and Oaxaca. To avoid such a fate, a number of Yaquis fled to the Sonoran mountains or north to the United States. Today, there are 5,000 to 6,000 Yaquis in Arizona. They live in several towns south of Phoenix (for example, Chandler, Coolidge, and Florence) and just outside Tucson in the village of Pascua on some 202 acres deeded to them by the U.S. government in 1964. The Yaqui speak a dialect of Cahitan.

A Note

There are other Native American peoples who live in the geographical Southwest, in particular the Southern Paiute (in southeastern Nevada, southeastern California, and northern Arizona) and the Ute (in northernmost New Mexico and in Utah). But because anthropologists consider these peoples to belong to the culture area of the Great Basin rather than that of the Southwest, they are outside the scope of this guide.

5

SOUTHWESTERN
ARTS AND CRAFTS

It has been said that when it comes to Native American arts and crafts, the Southwest is one of the richest culture areas of the continent. The variety of the objects made, the materials utilized, the techniques used in their production, the forms these objects take, and the designs that embellish them are very rich indeed. Among the items produced are pottery drums and two-headed wooden drums; decorated flutes and rattles; beaded bags, necklaces, and cradleboards; skin dresses, saddle bags, and moccasins; hide shields; baskets and clayware of various types; many items of silver jewelry, some set with gemstones; wood carvings; woven articles such as rugs, blankets, and sashes; sandpaintings; and recently even easel paintings.

Most of the skills Native Americans used in producing these objects were acquired long before their first contact with Europeans. Some of the items were originally made primarily for ceremonial use (for example, rattles and certain baskets). Others were designed and made to serve practical purposes (for example, pottery and saddle bags). But in no case was their aesthetic appearance neglected, and there were never any copies, only originals. And because many of the native artists and craftspeople have been not only eager to perpetuate their traditional designs but also willing to respond to the tastes and needs of the wider society, the variety of forms and designs available today is remarkable.

Visitors and those living in the Southwest are fortunate to have the opportunity to acquire exquisite pieces of Native

American art directly from their makers or from museum shops, galleries, trading posts, and many other reliable retailers. What follows is a brief discussion of the best-known types of Native Southwestern art—Navajo weaving, silverwork, basketry, Pueblo pottery, and kachina dolls. (The spelling *katsina* has recently come into use to designate Hopi supernatural beings and the dancers who represent them because it more clearly resembles the way Hopis pronounce the word, but the common English spelling *kachina* is still used to designate the dolls.)

Navajo Weaving

According to the Navajo, their women learned how to weave from Spider Woman, and how to make a loom from Spider Man. Some students of Navajo culture accept the possibility that the Navajo may have been familiar with weaving when they came to the Southwest from the north, where weaving was done by some Native Americans before the arrival of Europeans. But anthropologists generally believe that the Navajo learned to weave from the Pueblos after they arrived in the Southwest. A particularly good opportunity would have existed a decade or so after the Pueblo Revolt of 1680, when the Spaniards regained control of the area. At that point many Pueblos sought refuge from the Spanish by moving north into Navajo country or by actually living among the Navajo. In any case, the earliest historical references, dating from the very beginning of the eighteenth century, stated that the Navajo wove their clothes of wool obtained from the flocks of sheep that they raised.

Among the several methods of weaving used by the Navajo over the years, the simplest and most widespread has been the plain tapestry method. Some Navajo women have used the more complicated twilling, a method commonly applied to saddle blankets because it produces pieces that are thicker and more durable than those made by plain weaving. Only a very few weavers are still able to do double-faced, or two-faced, weaving, in which each of the two sides of a woven piece has an entirely different pattern.

The sources of color the Navajo have used through the years are of three main types—natural, vegetable, and aniline. Al-

Navajo woman at a loom. Weaving techniques and the vertical loom were probably borrowed from the Pueblo several centuries ago and have been used to the present day with little or no modification. Courtesy of Museum of Northern Arizona Photo Archives (E203B. 36/83.0128). Photo by M. Middleton.

though the natural colors of the wool are limited to white, brown, brownish black, tan, and gray, vegetable dyes made from various plants range through many shades of pastels: for example, soft brown from the bark of alder, light gray from the berries of ironwood, reddish purple from the roots of wild plum, bluish black from the leaves of sumac, tan from the blossoms of Indian paintbrush, light yellow from the flowers of wild celery, and so on. Dyes from pulverized minerals are also used. In the past 100 years or so wool for rugs has often been colored with aniline dyes, which produce colors much brighter than either the vegetable dyes or the chrome dyes (dyes applied with a chromium compound as the mordant).

To make a Navajo blanket or rug is painstaking work. For those who still process their own wool, it begins in the spring with shearing the sheep and washing and drying the fleece. Next comes the carding of the wool, after which it must be spun into yarn. Finally the wool is dyed. Before actual weaving can begin, the warp must be carefully strung and the loom set up. Careful estimates made in 1973 established that a three-by-five rug of above-average quality, from the catching of the sheep to the handing over of the finished rug at the trading post, required close to 400 hours of the weaver's time. Although trading-post rug prices may appear to be high, most people would consider the compensation the weaver receives as totally inadequate for the time and effort that must be expended.

Those who have studied the history of Navajo weaving distinguish three main periods. During the first—the classic period, until about 1865—Navajo women wove clothing for their own use and the use of their families—especially poncholike dresses, shoulder blankets (blankets for wearing), and men's shirts. During the transition period—from about 1865 until the 1890s—the weaving of blankets gave way to the making of rugs for trade. Innovations included the use of manufactured yarns, commercial dyes, and elaborate and colorful "eye-dazzler" designs. And during the rug period that followed—from about 1895 until the present—most Navajo weaving has been market oriented, although some items continue to be made for use by the Navajos themselves, especially saddle blankets.

The style of blankets, and later of rugs, during the several centuries these two have been woven by the Navajo, has changed from traditional symmetrical and angular designs (stripes, terraced design, diamonds) to designs catering to the tastes of the non-Navajo who buy the rugs. The design of many of the early blankets (rugs) was influenced by the Mexican weaving center in Saltillo, Mexico, which most often made use of a large diamond-shaped design with serrated outline. Some of the modern rugs, however, use pictorial designs or mythological motifs. But rugs with identical designs do not exist because the design is in the weaver's head and takes shape only as a piece is woven.

One particular type of traditional Navajo blanket that developed from men's shoulder blankets deserves special mention—the chief blankets, so called because they were sold or traded to other tribes in the Southwest and the Great Plains and worn by chiefs or others who could afford them. In the earliest phase of these blankets, up until about 1850, the typical design was of parallel stripes running along the length of the blanket in natural white, black, and indigo blue. During the next one or two decades, this design was enhanced by red bars woven into the centers and edges of the blue stripes. These red bars were made out of bright red yarn that had been unraveled and respun from a flannel manufactured in England and obtained from Mexico, where it had arrived by way of Spain. During the last phase, from around the 1870s, a diamond with serrate edge was woven into the center of the striped background and half or quarter diamonds into the corners and along the edges of the blanket.

Because the Navajo Indian Reservation is quite large—larger than the Commonwealth of Massachusetts—its various areas have developed regional styles of rug designs. In recent years some of these styles have begun to transcend their original localities and can be found in other areas of the reservation. Among the best-known regional styles are those from Wide Ruins (Arizona), having no border designs and making use of soft vegetable colors; Two Gray Hills (New Mexico), which are tightly woven and use natural-color fibers and intricate, frequently geometric designs with several borders; Crystal (New Mexico), known for striped rugs with no borders, often with soft colors derived from vegetable dyes; and Teec Nos Pos (Arizona), which employ wide borders, frequently with diamond designs in the center and an outline of a different color around the many decorative elements. Some styles are even identifiable as originating with particular families.

Some rugs woven in the western parts of the reservation make use of what is known as the storm pattern. These rugs favor the use of white, black, gray, and red and feature a rectangle woven in the center from which emanate lightning bolts, represented by zigzag lines. Small rectangles usually decorate the corners of the rug. Other designs depict gods *(yeis)* or masked dancers *(yeibichais)* like those seen in Navajo dry paintings. These are made primarily in the Chinle (Arizona) and Shiprock (New Mexico) areas. And then there are the so-called eye-dazzler rugs, with busy multicolor designs of triangles and diamonds with saw-toothed outlines, pictorial rugs depicting the things the weavers see around them such as hogans, mountains, horses, birds, sheep, trees, trucks, locomotives, railroad cars, or planes, and most recently even rugs with designs based on fantasy, such as Jurassic Park–style dinosaurs. In fact, a number of contemporary students of Navajo weaving have observed enough new trends during the past 40 or so years to justify speaking of a fourth period, the recent. It is during this period that some of the most creative and skillful weavers, whose works are especially sought, have begun to "sign" their rugs or tapestries by weaving their initials into one corner.

Buying a Rug: How to Make a Wise Purchase

Potential buyers of a Navajo rug will of course want to exercise their own taste and judgment in choosing a rug, particularly when it comes to design and color scheme. But to ensure the purchase of a rug of good quality, some advice may be helpful. Open the rug fully and lay it out flat on the floor to establish that it has no wrinkles, the corners are square, the weave is tight and consistent, and the colors and thickness of the weave are uniform. Examine both sides of the rug and make sure that both end edges are equally wide, the lines of the design straight and uniformly wide, and the entire design symmetrical. High-quality Navajo rugs have been a good investment for years now, but those interested in investing in one or more should beware of rather good imitations. Buyers are well advised to purchase Navajo rugs directly from the weavers themselves or from reputable sources such as museum shops, established trading posts, or well-known retailers of Navajo rugs.

Kachina Dolls

The term *kachina doll* is something of a misnomer because kachina dolls do not serve as playthings but are representations of katsina dancers, who in turn are masked human impersonators of the many supernatural beings of the Hopi religion. The figurines are referred to in English as kachina *dolls* rather than as simply *kachinas* to differentiate them from the katsinas themselves (the supernatural beings) as well as from katsina dancers.

The Hopi have been carving the predecessors of modern kachina dolls for many centuries. Although katsina dancers performed their ceremonial dances in the Hopi villages even before the Spanish conquest, specimens of early kachina dolls are very rare because wood, from which most of these early figurines were carved, is a material that under normal circumstances decays over time. The oldest known wooden kachina dates back only to about 1850, but representations of kachina dolls can be seen in murals found in a number of ruins as well as on pottery from much earlier times. Prehistoric kachina-like figures carved from stone have also been found. All of these early pieces are rudimentary in form. Even the dolls made only 100 years ago are quite simple. Whether large or small, they are round, or flat with rounded edges, and are quite stylized. Arms are usually indicated but are not separated from the torso.

Kachina dolls traditionally have been made from the roots of dead cottonwood trees. Large cottonwoods are preferred because the larger the root, the larger and more valued the kachina doll that can be carved from it. If the root happens to be damp, or partially green, then it must be thoroughly dried and seasoned. Because over the many years of kachina doll carving the supply of suitable cottonwood roots near the Hopi villages has been depleted, and a change in the weather patterns during the first third of this century wiped out the cottonwood trees along the nearby drainages, Hopi carvers must go much farther afield to gather the roots themselves or buy them from sources in other parts of the Southwest. Cottonwood root is used because it is the respected traditional material, is light in weight, can be easily carved, and does not easily dent. The use of other woods has not proved satisfactory. For example, balsa wood is too soft, pine too hard (and it tends to crack), and cedar too dark in color.

In the course of the twentieth century, kachina dolls have become more and more elaborate. Contemporary ones, intricately carved and carefully painted, are usually quite realistic. For the most part, they are no longer static but are carved to portray katsina dancers in action. Unlike a generation ago, most large dolls are now made from only one piece of wood, including arms and some parts of the costume. Pieces of gear (most kachinas hold something in both hands—for example, bows and arrows, crooks, rattles) are carved separately and then attached to the doll's body with pegs and glue. The figurines are sanded well, and then, to seal the pores of the wood, they are primed with a thin wash of clay.

For the painting process, mineral and vegetable dyes were used on early kachina dolls. During the twentieth century, carvers have used poster paints, later casein paints, and most recently acrylics. Today, acrylic paints are used on almost all dolls, although recently some makers have been experimenting with oil paints and pigmented stains. In addition to paint, dolls are often embellished with shells, leather, fur, painted cloth, wool yarn, bits of silver, and feathers. In the past, the feathers used were those left over from village ceremonies and came from eagles, falcons, red-tailed hawks, owls, or crows. Now that some of these species are protected, feathers used for the dolls must come from domestic fowl, pheasants, pigeons, and the like. Some prizewinning kachina dolls have been enhanced by the use of an electric wood-burning iron to make the shafts and barbs of carved feathers and the wrinkles on faces and hands appear more realistic.

Among recent innovations in the production of kachina dolls are kachina sculptures. Except for the head and head ornamentation, kachina sculptures are usually unpainted and, to preserve the natural elongated shape of the root, uncarved. Other innovations include miniature kachina dolls as well as figurines having nothing to do with the traditional katsina dancers that appear in Hopi plazas at ceremonial times. However, out of respect for tradition, one of the older carvers always combined

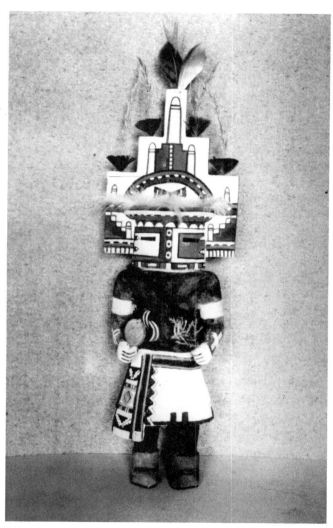

Hemis, or Niman, kachina doll of the Hopi, representing a katsina dancer who participates in the July ceremonies that mark the return of the katsinas to their home in the San Francisco Peaks near Flagstaff. Note the elaborate tableta, painted with fertility symbols, above the helmet mask. Courtesy of Museum of Northern Arizona Photo Archives (E111H.5A/10284).

the characteristics of several katsina types on the dolls he carved for sale so that his commercial dolls could not be taken to represent a particular katsina.

In traditional kachina dolls, color indicates which of the six cardinal directions the katsina has come from. Yellow stands for north or northwest, blue-green for west or southwest, red for south or southeast, white for east or northeast, black for zenith or above, and nadir or below is multicolored. The color of the doll's head and body indicates whether the spirit represented is benevolent or dangerous.

Hopi carvers used to be exclusively men and remained anonymous, but in recent years women have also begun to carve the dolls, and now many makers initial the stand or a foot of the larger figures. Originally, kachina dolls were not for sale. They were, and are, given to Hopi infants, both male and female, and to young girls during ceremonies. Then, because females have no part in the katsina rituals, the dolls are hung on the walls in Hopi houses to help women and young girls establish a feeling of kinship with the katsinas.

Since shortly after World War II the carving of kachina dolls has become an increasingly popular source of cash income as well as of traditional ceremonial gifts. Some carvers are even beginning to specialize, carving only certain types of dolls—the mudhead, for example. Most kachina dolls are between 8 and 15 inches in height, but miniature ones are only a few inches, and the largest can be several feet tall. Although there are non-Pueblo imitators who make carvings that resemble kachina dolls, the true dolls made by the Hopi are unsurpassed.

Given the several hundred different types of dolls, each identified by name, efforts have been made by anthropologists and museum curators to classify them. One approach has been to group the dolls according to the function of the katsina spirits they represent—for example, chiefs, clowns, runners, participants in the Bean Ceremony held in February, those that appear with female katsinas (impersonated by men) during one-day ceremonies, and so on. Some of the dolls are limited to a certain Hopi mesa or to a single village. Others are found on all three of the Hopi mesas. Some of the older kachina dolls fall out of use and new ones are introduced. The extent to which the physical characteristics of a particular kachina doll can be changed is very limited: the gear may be enhanced but must be of the proper kind, and the position of the figure and the arrangement of the costume can vary only slightly.

Several books are available that describe the principal features of kachina dolls and provide keys to their identification—for example, the masks and costumes they wear and the features on the top or sides of their heads (bird wings, horns, snout, beard, feathers, and many other features that are carved, painted, or attached). All kachinas have Hopi names, of course, but only some of them can be referred to by an English translation. The wide variety of kachinas may best be illustrated by a small sampling of their English names: Death Fly kachina, Broad-Faced kachina, Warrior kachina, White Ogre kachina, Disheveled kachina, Cumulus Cloud kachina, Snow kachina, Crazy Rattle kachina, Chipmunk kachina, Dung Carrier kachina, Mudhead kachina, Three-Horned kachina, Hummingbird kachina, Wolf kachina, Sunset Crater kachina, and Left-Handed kachina.

Buying a Kachina Doll

Anyone who plans to buy a kachina doll is advised to look for one that has good bodily proportions, is carved in detail, and has been painted with care and skill. A traditional doll is never one that is covered with large amounts of fur or dangling attachments. Whether purchasing a doll from the carver or a shop, the buyer should ask that the doll be identified by name—for example, Squash kachina, Buffalo kachina, or Roadrunner kachina. In the case of good pieces, the buyer should request the name of the carver, the village he or she comes from, and the date the carving was made.

One of the popular kachina dolls is the Wolf kachina. As side dancers, Wolf katsinas usually accompany the Cow, Deer, or Mountain Sheep katsina dancers impersonating plant-eating animals. They also occasionally appear in mixed dances, dances in which a number of different types of katsinas are impersonated. The Wolf kachina doll is characterized by a snout with teeth, yellow body paint, breech clout, red yarn skirt, and red moccasins. Forearms and the legs below the knees are painted with white or black spots.

Southwestern Silverwork

Native Americans are very good with their hands, and those who have made their home in the Southwest are particularly versatile and creative craftspeople. During prehistoric times they used shell, bone, and horn as well as different kinds of stone to make various items of personal adornment, among them bracelets, rings, pendants, and hairpins. They made beads (some extremely tiny) from turquoise, jet, and argillite as well as shells; cut or carved pendants representing various animals (birds, toads, and others) from shell or stone; and overlaid shells with turquoise. The Franciscan priest Marcos de Niza, who visited what is now the U.S. Southwest in 1539, a year before Coronado's expedition, commented on the large amount of turquoise worn as ornaments, with some people wearing as many as four strings of turquoise around their necks and others using pieces of turquoise as ear pendants and nose ornaments.

Metalworking among the Native Americans of the Southwest is of relatively recent origin. In the 1830s both Navajo and Zuni men reportedly began using copper and brass to make jewelry for the Mexicans, who brought these metals north with them. By about 1850 at least some Native Americans had learned from the Mexicans to work iron, and during the 1860s the Navajos interned at Fort Sumner hammered copper and brass into bracelets. Although the Navajo had been fond of wearing silver for years, they did not learn silversmithing from wandering Mexican *plateros* (silversmiths) until about 1870. The Zuni in turn learned it from one of the first Navajo silversmiths just a few years later. The skill of silversmithing spread to several other Pueblo peoples before the end of the nineteenth century, the Hopi learning it from a Zuni silversmith in the 1890s. Until about 1890 the main source of silver was American silver dollars. Then for some 40 years Mexican silver coins were used. During the 1930s Native American silversmiths began buying silver slugs and later sheet silver to use in their work.

The best-known silversmiths today are the Navajo, the Hopi, and the Zuni, although other Pueblo villagers—those from Acoma, Laguna, Isleta, and Santo Domingo, for example—also do good work. The early silver objects made by the Navajo were either plain or very simply decorated with the use of an

Massive Navajo silver bracelets and belt buckles. Such jewelry, cast or hammered, is widely used throughout the Southwest by both Native Americans and others. Courtesy of Museum of Northern Arizona Photo Archives (E207.19/10672).

awl, but before long the Navajo began to embellish them with designs stamped in with the iron punches used to decorate leather. The use of stones—turquoise, native garnets, malachite, jet, and others—was initiated in the 1880s; before the end of the nineteenth century, turquoise won out over the other stones and by the beginning of the twentieth century came to be used in ever-increasing quantities. Several other methods were added to working silver—soldering, repoussage (hammering or pressing out a design from the reverse side), and sand casting (in sandstone molds), in particular—and today the variety of the types of jewelry made for sale is astonishing. Whether of silver only, or silver set with stones, Navajo silverwork today includes anklets, armlets, buttons, bracelets, necklaces, rings, earrings, hair clips, wristwatch bands, tie clasps, neckerchief slides, pins, brooches, pendants (especially the crescent-shaped *najas*), bolo ties, hatbands, belt buckles, money clips, concha belts, and wrist guards, worn to protect the inner surface of an archer's wrist from a recoiling bowstring. The so-called squash-blossom necklaces have become a particularly popular item among those who enjoy wearing Southwestern jewelry.

Although much of the silver jewelry produced during the twentieth century has been for the tourist trade, the Native Americans of the Southwest also make it for their own use and enjoyment. Much of the silverwork is done by men, but some years ago women began to involve themselves in the work—setting stones, grinding and polishing, and working silver—and by now have become jewelry makers in their own right.

Among the Zuni, who like to set turquoise in silver, silver jewelry is less massive than the jewelry made by the Navajo. Zuni women have become expert in stone cutting and mounting. One of the favorite designs used by the Zuni is the cluster— a number of small pieces of turquoise usually arranged around a larger center piece. A great many very small stones attractively set is referred to as needlepoint style.

The Hopi make very little use of stones and tend to decorate their silver with the traditional designs used in their weaving and on their pottery. Their specialty is silver overlay: A design is cut out from a piece of silver, the piece is then soldered onto a matching solid piece of silver, and the design area is oxidized to show up black against the polished surroundings.

The success of Southwestern jewelry has encouraged assembly-line production, even among some Native Americans. During the past three decades commercial jewelry-making machinery has found its way onto the Navajo Reservation. The discriminating visitor to the Southwest is likely to prefer to buy jewelry made by a single craftsperson if for no other reason than the tendency of Native American artists never to make pieces that are identical to each other.

When a Navajo occasionally needs to borrow money, he or she may pawn a piece of jewelry with a trader. Such an item must be kept by the trader for the period of time agreed upon so that the owner has an opportunity to redeem it. If the owner fails to do so, the pawn becomes "dead" and can then be sold. Of course both very good and below-average pieces of jewelry can become dead pawn, and the price at which a pawn piece can be purchased may or may not be to the buyer's advantage.

Southwestern Basketry

Basket weaving in the Southwest is a skill that goes back at least 8,000 years. In the past, baskets served both ceremonial and utilitarian functions and were indispensable before pottery was made. In modern times, when inexpensive factory-made containers can easily replace baskets that would take a great deal of time to weave by hand, the craft of basket making among many Native Americans has almost disappeared. In the Southwest, however, the interest of both tourists and residents in well-crafted baskets has stimulated some Native Americans to continue making them, improving upon a skill their people have been developing over many centuries and supplementing traditional forms and designs with new ones.

The plants used in basketwork have varied depending on the types available in the area of the Southwest where particular basket weavers live and whether the materials are to be used for the more stationary warp or the more supple weft. Plant materials have included withes, stems, leaves, or roots—of willow, cottonwood, acacia, devil's claw, cattail, yucca, mountain mahogany, sumac, squawberry, rabbitbrush, and still other plants. Some of these also provide the desirable natural colors used in the design—for example, from devil's claw, the black, and from yucca, mountain mahogany, and sumac, the reddish brown.

The types of basket weaving used in the Southwest are wickerwork, coiling, and plaiting. All three go back to prehistoric times, and to varying degrees all are still in use today. In plain wickerwork, the more pliable weft is woven under and over the stiffer warp. To produce stronger and more elaborate baskets, the weft is wrapped around each warp to make wrapped wicker (or wrappedwork); working with two wefts at a time, passing them alternately over and under each warp, results in twined wicker; and still other variations of wickerwork can be used.

In plaited baskets, warps and wefts are usually of the same material, with both much wider than they are thick. The strips of material pass over and under each other (plain plaiting) or over and under more than one strip at a time (twilled plaiting). Coiling, the most widely used technique in the Southwest, involves wrapping the weft around the warp, which begins at the center of the bottom and moves spirally out to the rim of the basket, and then piercing holes in the coil by means of an awl, inserting the weft through the holes, and sewing neighboring coils together. The technique of coiling is especially suitable for imaginative designs.

Among modern Native Americans of the Southwest, with only a few exceptions, the weavers of baskets have been women. Many of the different basket-weaving peoples have preferred one or another technique, and originally some made baskets of only a particular functional type (or types), which resulted in intertribal trading for the types a group did not make themselves. The Jicarilla Apache and the Navajo, for example, are known for coiled baskets, the San Juan people for wickerwork. Some, like the Hopi, have long been expert in all three. Since the beginning of the twentieth century the Hopi have become somewhat specialized according to the particular mesa they are from. The Hopi villages on Second Mesa are widely known for their coiled basketry, those on Third Mesa for their wickerwork (and all Hopi villages make plaited yucca "sifter" baskets for winnowing seeds and grains). The Western Apache have been known for their burden baskets, the Yavapai for dippers, the Jemez for yucca wheat-washing baskets, and the Papago for storage jars—to mention only a few examples.

The variety of forms in Southwestern basketry includes plaques, trays, bowls, creels, water "bottles" (tightly woven baskets coated inside with melted piñon pitch), jars, hats, hampers, and burden carriers. More recently, lidded pieces and life-form

Hopi coiled plaque from Second Mesa. Courtesy of Museum of North-ern Arizona Photo Archives (E104C.44/73.2522). Coiled plaque, Martha Laban; photo by Marc Gaede.

baskets (shaped as humans, dogs, owls, for example) have been added. Each of these occurs in several variants. Jars are made, for example, with large or small mouth, longer, shorter, or no neck, lean or spherical body, and so on. The size of modern baskets made for sale can vary from miniature to several feet in height.

Decorations range from traditional geometric designs using straight, perpendicular, or curved lines, to star and flowerlike themes, to representations of life forms—eagles, butterflies, turtles, sunflowers, and others. As on pottery, the number of colors on any given basket is usually limited to three or four. Sources of the colors are most often still natural, but aniline dyes have also been used for over a century now.

Choosing a Basket

With the wide selection of Native American baskets available in the Southwest, what should a buyer look for? Once again, the buyer's taste and the uses planned for the item will determine the shape and design, but there are certain general characteristics that make some baskets more desirable than others. Fine material used as weft is preferable to coarse material; the ribs passing over and under the warps should be even and straight; the entire rim should be of the same thickness and carefully finished; and natural colors have softer tones than aniline or other commercial dyes.

Pueblo Pottery

The technology of pottery making was known to the Anasazi, the ancestors of the modern Pueblo peoples, by about A.D. 500. The skill most likely had spread north from the peoples who lived south of the Anasazi. Designs on early vessels were geometrical, with black used as the decorative color, leading to the descriptive terms black-on-white or black-on-gray. During the centuries that followed, innovations included new vessel forms, asymmetrical designs, use of several colors, stippling, and engraving. Some examples date back to the fifteenth and sixteenth centuries.

When the cross-continental railroad was completed in the Southwest during the 1880s and inexpensive china and metal wares became available, in some Pueblo villages pottery making declined, but in others traditional pottery began to be produced for sale to non-Indians who appreciated its beauty. Today in a number of Pueblo villages either pottery making is no longer a viable activity or if it has continued, it is undistinguished. In several, however, it has retained its traditional aesthetic character, and representative pieces are now collected by major museums as well as by discriminating individuals who appreciate both creativity and superior craftsmanship.

Among the Western Pueblo peoples, modern Hopi pottery is probably the best known and of the highest quality. Before 1300, Hopi pottery was simply one of the many regional varieties in the Pueblo area. During the fourteenth century the Hopi, in a spurt of creativity, began to make use of black-on-orange and black-on-yellow designs, and by the addition of red began producing polychromes—earthenware decorated in three or more colors. The earlier geometric patterns used on Pueblo pottery were enriched by the addition of curvilinear designs representing such forms as flowers, birds, butterflies, and humans. The best-known specimens of this type of pottery were excavated during the 1890s in the prehistoric Hopi site of Sikyatki on First Mesa. Pieces of the modern version of Sikyatki polychrome are characterized by highly stylized life forms against a yellow background.

Although men may occasionally assist with decorating the pieces, Hopi potters are women. They obtain the clay below the mesas, soak it, knead it, add grit (sand, ground-up potsherds) if necessary, and then mix it with water. Larger pieces are made by coiling—attaching a roll of clay to a flat round clay base and then coiling the roll spirally upward to the desired height. The curving, thinning, and smoothing of the walls is done with pieces of gourd and sandstone. After further smoothing with a pebble, the surface is covered with slip, a thin clay-based wash (unless the walls of the piece can be polished and painted without slipping), and then decorated. Black pigment is generally obtained either by boiling tansy mustard leaves, pouring off the water, and squeezing the remaining pulp through cloth, or from black, fine-grained soft rocks ground and mixed with water. The resulting thick black liquid can be used immediately or preserved in dry cakes. For white, the potters use a fine white clay that they mix with water, and for yellow, a clay containing iron hydroxide. Firing is done in the open, with dry sheep manure and occasionally native coal added to the wood fire. Temperature and length of firing must be carefully watched to prevent cracking, uneven or spotted coloring, or smudging.

Hopi potters still produce simple utilitarian wares (cooking vessels, storage jars, and canteens), but it is the decorated wares that are appreciated by collectors all over the world. The best-known pottery comes from the villages of Hano, Sichomovi, and Walpi, on First Mesa. The bowls are usually decorated on the inside, the jars on the outside. Whether the designs feature katsinas, flowers, bird beaks, eyes, feathers, and tails or geomet-

Hopi bowl from First Mesa, decorated in several colors. The design uses both curved and straight lines. Courtesy of Museum of Northern Arizona Photo Archives (E105.469/77.0331).

ric and angular elements, they are well proportioned and finely finished. The designs are painted directly on the pottery without the potter's having sketched them in.

Other Native American peoples of the Southwest also make pottery, and several of them have gained a national and even international reputation. Among the Eastern Pueblo peoples (those living in New Mexico), at the least the following deserve to be mentioned: the people of Santa Clara for their polished black pottery as well as polychromes and incised or carved designs, including incised miniatures; the San Ildefonsans, known for polished black-on-black (black matte against polished black) as well as polychrome ware, and also for carved and incised designs; and the people of San Juan for polished redware and incised designs painted with clays of different colors—brick-red, lime-white, gray, tan, and others. In addition to these three Pueblo peoples and the Hopi, over a dozen other Pueblo villages are known for their pottery. Among the non-Pueblo peoples, the Maricopa, Mohave, Papago, and Navajo also make pottery.

Buying Southwestern Pottery

When buying one of these handsome ceramic pieces made by the Pueblos, look for symmetry of form, thin walls, a smooth surface, clear colors, and a balanced design carefully executed. To avoid hidden cracks, strike the piece gently; it should ring like a bell. For some time now many potters have been signing the bottoms of their pieces, sometimes also giving their village and the date when the piece was made. Because there are imitations for sale that are not made by Native Americans, it is wise to buy pottery either directly from the potters in the villages or from established trading posts, museum shops, or arts and craft centers that guarantee the authenticity of what they offer for sale.

Scores of Southwestern Native American potters are well known by name and make exquisite pieces that can command very high prices. So many potters have distinguished themselves that to give specific names would run the risk of omitting others who are equally deserving.

6

▣ PREHISTORIC MONUMENTS ▣ IN THE SOUTHWEST

In this chapter we will briefly describe the most important prehistoric sites in the Southwest. To aid the readers who may be visiting only a portion of the area, we list the national monuments and parks according to states (Arizona, Colorado, New Mexico, and Utah) and alphabetically within each state. In addition we have numbered the sites consecutively and indicated on the map the approximate location of each.

To supplement the information offered here, visitors are encouraged to ask for the free brochures or inexpensive pamphlets available in the visitor centers. Most visitor centers have bookstores and offer museum exhibits illustrative of the material culture of the prehistoric inhabitants of the particular area. A brief discussion of the Ancestral Puebloans (Anasazi), Sinagua, Hohokam, and other prehistoric peoples is in Chapter 2, "Prehistory of the Southwest."

Arizona

1. Canyon de Chelly National Monument

The name Canyon de Chelly (pronounced d'SHAY) probably derives through Spanish from the Navajo word *tsegi,* meaning "rock canyon." Canyon de Chelly belongs to the Navajo Nation, on whose land it is located, but it is administered by the National Park Service. The entrance to the canyon and the visi-

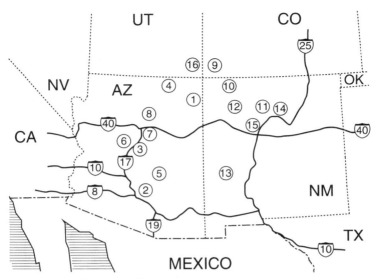

Approximate locations of the national parks and monuments described in this chapter, by identifying number, in relation to the interstate highway system

tor center are located at Chinle, two miles east of U.S. Highway 191, in the northeastern corner of Arizona.

Canyon de Chelly and its major tributary Canyon del Muerto have been inhabited for at least 2,000 years. Early inhabitants were the Ancestral Puebloans (or Anasazi, from a Navajo word meaning "alien" or "enemy ancestors"), whose culture reached its peak during the eleventh, twelfth, and thirteenth centuries. By 1300 the Ancestral Puebloans had almost completely abandoned the canyon. Several centuries later, about 1600, the Navajo began arriving from the north and east. Several hundred Navajos still consider the canyon their home. Some continue living in traditional hogans, care for their sheep, and plant corn, squash, and other crops each spring. Most Navajo people are bicultural: They continue to practice and teach Navajo traditions and values while living in present-day American society.

Canyon de Chelly and Canyon del Muerto are known for their many archaeological sites such as White House, Antelope House, Mummy Cave, and Standing Cow as well as the many early Puebloan and Navajo pictographs. The canyons are also famous for spectacular geological formations such as 800-foot-high Spider Rock rising from the canyon floor.

For the Navajo people, the two canyons have a bitter historical significance. In a rock shelter (later to become known as Massacre Cave) in Canyon del Muerto, more than 100 Navajos, including 25 women and children, were massacred by the Spaniards in 1805. Then in 1864 a detachment of cavalrymen under Kit Carson rounded up Navajo warriors in the canyons, destroyed their livestock and several thousand peach trees, burned their homes, and marched 1,500 Navajos from the canyons to Fort Sumner, New Mexico, where they were interned for five long years.

The only access into Canyon de Chelly for visitors on their own is a 2.5-mile trail (round-trip) from the rim drive down to White House Ruin, the best-known site in the area. Those who do not wish to hike that distance down into the canyon and back can either take the north and/or the south rim drive (each 36 miles round-trip) with overlooks along the edge of the canyon, or sign up for half-day or daylong canyon tours in open trucks with Navajo driver-guides. These can be arranged for through Thunderbird Lodge in Chinle (tel. 520-674-5841).

For more information, write to Superintendent, Canyon de Chelly National Monument, P.O. Box 588, Chinle, AZ 86503, or telephone 520-674-5500. The visitor center is open from 8 A.M. to 6 P.M. in the summer, 8 A.M. to 5 P.M. in the winter. Campsites are available on a first-come, first-served basis. Motel accommodations, stores, and restaurants can be found in nearby Chinle. Note that Canyon de Chelly National Monument, in contrast to the rest of Arizona, observes daylight saving time because it is on the Navajo Reservation.

2. Casa Grande Ruins National Monument

Casa Grande Ruins National Monument is just off State Highway 87/287 on the northern edge of Coolidge, about 20 miles northeast of Casa Grande. The main feature of the prehistoric village built by the Hohokam around 1350 is a four-story structure, the Casa Grande, "great house" in Spanish. The walls of this building are deeply entrenched in the ground and over four feet thick at their base. They were built primarily from a natural substance found four to five feet below ground level—a mixture of sand, clay, and limestone that dries as hard as brick. Archaeologists are still not certain what purpose the large building served. Among the functions that have been suggested are a residence for a chief or priests, an astronomical observatory, and a communal storage area.

The Hohokam were efficient builders and farmers. They surrounded their village with a high wall and irrigated their farmlands outside the village by means of canals that drew their water from the Gila River, a few miles away. Altogether, the irrigation system built by the Hohokam in the valleys of the Salt and Gila Rivers was between 600 and 1,000 miles in extent. Some excavated Hohokam canals were as wide as 10 feet and as deep as 8 feet. The villages in the Gila Valley had been abandoned by the middle of the fifteenth century for reasons not yet fully understood, but quite possibly climatic.

The monument is open year-round from 8 A.M. to 5 P.M., but closed on December 25. Some of the artifacts made by the Hohokam are on exhibit in the visitor center. For more information, write to Superintendent, Casa Grande Ruins National Monument, 1100 Ruins Drive, Coolidge, AZ 85228, or telephone 520-723-3172.

3. Montezuma Castle National Monument

Entry to Montezuma Castle National Monument is off Interstate 17 about 50 miles south of Flagstaff. Montezuma Well, a detached unit of the national monument that is well worth the additional time, is located 11 miles to the northeast. Both sites have short walking trails, and at Montezuma Castle the visitor center houses a small museum with information concerning the area.

According to one tradition, the name attached to both the "castle" and the "well" was given to them by early settlers of the Verde Valley who believed, incorrectly, that the imposing ruin was built by Aztec refugees who came north after their emperor, Montezuma, died in the custody of Hernando Cortes in 1520.

The five-story, twenty-room, structure, built into a cliff and accessible only by ladders, was begun by the Sinagua early in the twelfth century, after they had left the high country near today's Flagstaff. Here alongside Beaver Creek they found both a protected site for their home and water with which they could irrigate their crops of corn, beans, squash, and cotton, just as did their Hohokam neighbors to the south. Another source of water for small Sinagua groups moving south was the large limestone sinkhole with its natural spring now known as Montezuma Well, which provided not only water but also a few sites under the rim for living quarters. The conditions at these new locations of the Sinagua may have proved so attractive that those remaining in the higher elevations to the north began to migrate south, eventually overpopulating the area. The Sinagua left the valley in the early 1400s, some of them probably becoming absorbed by the pueblos to the north.

The monument is open year-round from 8 A.M. to 5 P.M. (7 P.M. during the summer). For more information, write to Superintendent, Montezuma Castle National Monument, P.O. Box 219, Camp Verde, AZ 86322, or telephone 520-567-3322.

4. Navajo National Monument

Navajo National Monument consists of three Ancestral Puebloan cliff villages, only two of which are now open to the public—Betatakin, "house on a rock ledge" in Navajo, and Keet Seel, "shattered house." The third and smallest, Inscription House, has been closed since 1968. The headquarters and visitor center are located close to Betatakin, the most accessible of the sites in the monument. Entrance is 9 miles up State Highway 564 from U.S. Highway 160, in the far northeastern part of Arizona, about 50 miles northeast of Tuba City or 20 miles southwest of Kayenta.

Navajo National Monument was established in 1909 to protect the ruins of Keet Seel. Inscription House and Betatakin were added after expeditions explored them the same year. The builders of the well-preserved cliff villages were the Kayenta Anasazi, one of the branches of the Ancestral Puebloan people. Construction dates from 1250 to about 1286, but these people had lived in the area for centuries before that time, farming in the canyon bottoms. Only two or, at the most, three generations of the Kayenta Anasazi enjoyed these remarkable villages. By about 1300 the inhabitants had left all three villages.

A partial view of Betatakin, a remarkably well-preserved
thirteenth-century cliff village in Navajo National Monument.
Courtesy of Museum of Northern Arizona Photo Archives
(MS122-2078). Photo by M. Applegate.

Betatakin, the smaller of the two ruins open to the public, can be viewed from the rim of the canyon along a one-mile round-trip foot trail. To go down into the village one must walk in with a ranger on scheduled hikes of about five hours round-trip. Walking back out of the canyon to the visitor center is about equal to climbing a 70-story building, and as the altitude of the monument is over 7,300 feet, the trip should not be undertaken by anyone with heart or respiratory problems.

Because Betatakin stands on solid bedrock in its alcove under the cliff, its two kivas were built above ground. Very thick masonry walls were used to approximate the underground effect. The dwellings could have housed about 125 people.

Keet Seel is one of the largest cliff villages in Arizona. It contains more than 150 rooms as well as several kivas and granaries, and at its peak, the population may have reached as many as 125 to 150 people. Besides the several types of rooms, the original inhabitants of Keet Seel also built a retaining wall up to 11 feet high that stretched in front of much of the village.

To visit Keet Seel one must obtain a special permit at the visitor center and then hike an arduous 17-mile round-trip trail. These trips are usually done as two-day backpacking trips and are limited to no more than 20 persons a day. Trips may be scheduled from Memorial Day weekend through Labor Day, and it is possible to make reservations up to two months prior to the date of the visit.

The monument is open year-round at 8 A.M., closing at 6 P.M. during the summer and earlier the rest of the year. Individual campsites are available on a first-come, first-served basis. Reservations can be made for group campsites. Neither food nor gasoline is available at the monument. Horseback tours to Keet Seel can be arranged at the visitor center. Visitors should keep in mind that, in contrast to the rest of Arizona, the Navajo Nation observes daylight saving time during the summer.

For more information, write to Superintendent, Navajo National Monument, HC 71, P.O. Box 3, Tonalea, AZ 86044-9704, or telephone 520-672-2366.

5. Tonto National Monument

Tonto National Monument is located east of Phoenix, below Theodore Roosevelt Lake, and is entered from State Highway 88 just east of the town of Roosevelt.

Between 1150 and the early 1400s, a people referred to by archaeologists as the Salado ("Salt people") farmed in this area, planting beans, corn, squash, and cotton in the Tonto Basin and irrigating their fields with ditches from the nearby Salt River. Apparently the prehistoric Salado culture originated along the Little Colorado River in what today is north-central Arizona. It was influenced by some of the major traditions of the Southwest—Mogollon, Anasazi, and Hohokam. The Salado were superb potters and fine weavers.

Sometime toward the end of the thirteenth century or the beginning of the fourteenth, some of the Salado moved to easily defensible cliff sites and built several villages in natural limestone alcoves. The stimulus for such building probably came from the Ancestral Puebloans to the north. The remains of two such villages can be seen in Tonto National Monument. To protect the upper village, consisting of 40 rooms, from further deterioration, it can only be visited in the company of a park ranger. The lower village can be reached by foot from the visitor center along a half-mile trail.

The Salado, like so many others, and for reasons that are not clear but have frequently been speculated on, left their villages around 1400. Some archaeologists believe that they migrated north and joined either the Hopi or the Zuni in their pueblos in what is now Arizona or New Mexico.

The monument is open year-round from 8 A.M. to 5 P.M. Ranger-conducted three-hour tours to less-accessible parts of the ruins are available from November through April. For more information, write to Superintendent, Tonto National Monument, P.O. Box 707, Roosevelt, AZ 85545, or telephone 520-467-2241.

6. *Tuzigoot National Monument*

Tuzigoot National Monument is located a few miles northwest of Cottonwood, through which runs U.S. 89A, an alternate route between Flagstaff and Prescott. Signs along 89A direct visitors to the national monument, which is near Clarkdale. Located on a hill about 120 feet above the Verde River, Tuzigoot, a Sinaguan village, was built between 1125 and 1400, but there is evidence of habitation in the 1000s. It was originally two stories high, with about 80 rooms on the ground floor. The name *Tuzigoot* means "crooked water" in Apache and apparently referred to the river and the lake area below.

The monument and its visitor center are open year-round from 8 A.M. to 5 P.M. (7 P.M. during the summer). For more information, write Tuzigoot National Monument, P.O. Box 68, Clarkdale, AZ 86324, or telephone 520-634-5564.

7. *Walnut Canyon National Monument*

The entrance to Walnut Canyon National Monument is a 3-mile paved road off Interstate 40, 7.5 miles east of Flagstaff. On a foot trail (0.75 miles) requiring a climb of 185 feet, one can walk alongside about 25 cliff dwelling "rooms" built into the side of the canyon. Many other prehistoric dwellings on the far side of the narrow canyon can also be seen from the trail. Visitors not wanting to undertake this trail can use the rim trail, which offers good views of the canyon and the cliff dwellings built into it. All these structures were built by the Sinagua between about 1125 and 1250. By about 1250 the prehistoric inhabitants of the canyon had moved southeast.

On the canyon rims, where sufficiently large pockets of suitable land could be found, the Sinagua grew their crops of corn, beans, and squash. Wild plants were also an important source of food, as were deer, bighorn sheep, rabbits, and various small mammals (more than twenty species of edible and medicinal plants still grow in the canyon). There is archaeological evidence that the Sinagua were active traders, exchanging food and distinctive pottery for semiprecious stones (turquoise, malachite, azurite, and others) used for ornaments, as well as seashells and macaw feathers. Some of these items came from areas around the Gulf of Mexico and the Gulf of California.

The monument is open year-round except December 25. Hours of operation are December through February, 9 A.M. to 5 P.M.; March through May and September through November, 8 A.M. to 5 P.M.; and June through August, 8 A.M. to 6 P.M. For more information, write to Superintendent, Walnut Canyon National Monument, Walnut Canyon Road, Flagstaff, AZ 86004, or telephone 520-526-3367.

8. Wupatki National Monument

Wupatki National Monument, with a number of prehistoric sites, is located about 25 miles north of Flagstaff. The entrance to Wupatki is off U.S. Highway 89. A 36-mile paved road off U.S. 89 runs through the monument, connects with Sunset Crater National Monument to the south, and then rejoins U.S. 89.

The eastern foothills of the San Francisco Peaks just north of Flagstaff were the home of prehistoric dry-land farming people, now called the Sinagua ("without water"), probably as early as the sixth century. Using runoff water, they irrigated their fields of corn, beans, and squash and supplemented these crops with wild plants and small game.

During the mid-1060s volcanic eruptions from what is now called Sunset Crater covered the ground with ash and cinders and forced the Sinagua to retreat south. But the area was resettled when it was discovered that the layer of volcanic debris helped the soil hold water and made the otherwise quick-drying earth more productive.

The Sinagua made baskets, pottery, and a variety of ornaments. From some of the other peoples who moved into the area from the west and northeast they learned how to build not only pueblos but also barriers designed to impound water. One structure located in the monument appears to have been a ball court very much like those used in southern Arizona and Mesoamerica—evidence of the influence of Mesoamerican cultures in the Southwest. Archaeologists have found trade objects at the monument coming from peoples living to the north, east, south, and west.

The largest ruin in the monument is called Wupatki, meaning "tall house" in the Hopi language. It may have contained as many as 100 rooms and housed as many as 200 people at the peak of its population. By about 1300 the Sinagua had left the area for lower elevations south of Flagstaff, perhaps due to the drought that affected a large part of the Southwest.

The monument and visitor center are open year-round from 8 A.M. to 5 P.M. except on Christmas Day. For more information, write to Superintendent, Wupatki–Sunset Crater–Walnut Canyon Headquarters, 2717 North Steves Boulevard, Suite 3, Flagstaff, AZ 86004, or telephone 520-556-7599.

Colorado

9. Mesa Verde National Park

Mesa Verde National Park is located in the high plateau country of the southwestern corner of Colorado. The entrance is about 1 mile south of U.S. Highway 160, 9 miles east of Cortez, and 6 miles west of Mancos. Mesa Verde covers an area of about 80 square miles, and the distance from the entrance to park headquarters and the three major cliff dwellings on Chapin Mesa is more than 20 miles. Even the most superficial viewing of some of the park's wonders requires at least half a day. Many visitors

Mesa Verde's Cliff Palace, the largest cliff dwelling in the Southwest and the best-known symbol of the Great Pueblo Period, A.D. 1100 to 1300, the golden age of the Anasazi (Ancestral Puebloan) culture. Courtesy of National Park Service.

may want to spend a full day or two, or even longer, taking advantage of all that Mesa Verde has to offer. The uniqueness of the park's treasures was recognized in 1978 when a branch of UNESCO designated Mesa Verde National Park as a World Heritage Cultural Site.

The estimated number of archaeological sites in Mesa Verde is 4,000, but only some, the most spectacular, are open to the public. On Chapin Mesa are Cliff Palace, Spruce Tree House, and Balcony House. On Wetherill Mesa are Step House and Long House. In addition, there are several hiking trails, such as the ones leading to Spruce Canyon from Chapin Mesa—Petroglyph Point Trail (2.8 miles) and Spruce Canyon Trail (2.1 miles).

The Ancestral Puebloan people first settled in Mesa Verde during the sixth century. They learned to make pottery and to farm, and they began using bows and arrows for hunting. They replaced their pithouses with houses above ground, and by about 1000 changed from adobe-and-pole construction to stone masonry. Most of the cliff dwellings preserved to the present were built during the early to mid-1200s. Cliff Palace had more than 200 rooms—not surprising, since the population of Mesa Verde may have reached several thousand by that time. Just as has been determined with respect to many other prehistoric villages of the Southwest, Mesa Verde was deserted by about 1300. Most likely drought and depletion of local resources—both animal and soil—were among the reasons, but there may have also been others. Some of the present-day Pueblo are likely the descendants of the Mesa Verde villagers.

Mesa Verde National Park is open year-round, but on a limited basis in the winter. During the summer, some of the best-known cliff villages are open on a self-guided basis, and there are ranger-guided tours throughout the year. Tickets for guided tours may be obtained at Far View Visitor Center. Five miles from the entrance to the park is Morefield Campground, open from April to October, with more than 500 sites providing all basic services. Chapin Mesa Museum has many exhibits explaining to visitors not only the human prehistory but also the natural history of the area.

For more information, write to Superintendent, Mesa Verde National Park, P.O. Box 8, Mesa Verde, CO 81330, or telephone 970-529-4461.

New Mexico

10. Aztec Ruins National Monument

Aztec Ruins National Monument is located in the northwestern corner of New Mexico off U.S. Highway 550 about one mile northwest of Aztec. The name *Aztec Ruins* was given to the monument by early settlers who mistakenly believed that the structure had been built by the Aztec people, conquered by Cortes in 1519.

Like so many archaeological monuments in the Southwest, this one too was built by the Ancestral Puebloans, in the early 1100s, and is believed to have served originally as a satellite community of Chaco Canyon to the south. Of particular interest is the reconstructed great kiva, the largest structure of its kind in the Southwest. The kiva was built by the first occupants, the Chacoan Anasazi, and then remodeled by the later group, the Mesa Verdean Anasazi. Both groups were attracted to this location by its fertile soil and the water supply from the Animas River. They cultivated the usual crops grown in the Southwest by prehistoric peoples—corn, squash, beans, and others.

Aztec was occupied twice during its two-century existence as a viable dwelling place. The settlement was among the largest in the prehistoric Southwest and at one time consisted of several pueblos. West Ruin was the largest, with about 400 rooms and many kivas. In places it was three stories high. As in so many other places, the inhabitants left the site at the end of the thirteenth century. Archaeologists assume that when the Ancestral Puebloans left the village, they joined other pueblos along the Rio Grande drainage and also in the Zuni and the Hopi areas. Much of the site at Aztec has not yet been excavated, and only a portion is open to the public.

The monument is open year-round from 8 A.M. to 5 P.M. (6 P.M. during summer) except for Thanksgiving, Christmas, and New Year's Day. At the entrance to the monument there is a visitor center with exhibits and a bookstore. Food and lodging are available in Aztec or Bloomfield, 8 miles south. For more information, write to Superintendent, Aztec Ruins National Monument, P.O. Box 640, Aztec, NM 87410-0640, or telephone 505-334-6174.

11. Bandelier National Monument

Bandelier National Monument owes its name to the Swiss-born anthropologist and historian Adolph Bandelier (1840–1914), who first viewed the site on October 23, 1880. "The grandest thing I ever saw," he recorded in his journal. The monument is located west of Santa Fe and south of Los Alamos. From Santa Fe it can be reached via U.S. Highway 285 north, State Highway 502 west, and then State Highway 4 south to the entrance.

Ancestral Puebloan peoples made their homes throughout the Pajarito Plateau, including Frijoles and other canyons, during the late 1100s and then moved out of the area in the early 1500s, leaving behind thousands of masonry structures. Two of

A view of Bandelier National Monument. Courtesy of National Park Service (#NPS 2949-1—Frame 10A). NPS photo by Fred Mang, Jr.

the best known are Long House Ruin and Tyuonyi, a circular two-story pueblo in the bottom of Frijoles Canyon. Both of these are within a half mile of the visitor center and can be reached by following the self-guided Main Loop Trail.

Among the archaeological sites visitors can see at Bandelier are Ceremonial Cave, 1 mile from the visitor center, and the detached Tsankawi section of the monument, 11 miles north of Frijoles Canyon along State Highway 4. Tsankawi includes a large unexcavated village on a mesa top overlooking the Rio Grande Valley and can be viewed from a 2-mile self-guided trail that for part of its way follows an ancient Indian trail worn deep into the soft volcanic rock.

Facilities at the monument include a campground on the mesa above Frijoles Canyon (95 campsites) and a picnic area along Frijoles Creek, as well as a snack bar and gift shop. The monument is open daily from dawn to dusk, the visitor center 8 A.M. to 6 P.M. from Memorial Day to Labor Day, and from 8 A.M. to 4:30 P.M. during the rest of the year. For more information, write to Superintendent, Bandelier National Monument, HCR 1, Box 1, Suite 15, Los Alamos, NM 87544, or telephone the visitor center at 505-672-3861. Recorded information is available twenty-four hours a day by calling 505-672-0343.

12. Chaco Culture National Historic Park

Chaco Culture National Historic Park, located in northwestern New Mexico, can be reached from State Highway 57 from the south and San Juan County road 7900 from the north. When traveling from the north, turn off State Highway 44 and follow county road 7900. When traveling from the south, take Exit 53 from Interstate 40 at Thoreau to State Highway 371 and proceed north through Crownpoint to State Highway 197 (also known as Navajo 9). After traveling 14 miles along 197, turn north on State Highway 57. Both northern and southern routes include about 20 miles of unpaved road, which can become impassable during bad weather. Visitors can call the park for road conditions.

The Anasazi ruins in the park go back to A.D. 850. Over 3,500 sites have been recorded within the boundaries of the park, and about 13 major ruins—multiroom and multistory pueblos. The best-known ruin is the D-shaped Pueblo Bonito, the size of which can best be appreciated by the length of the trail (0.6 mile) that leads through its two-acre site. By the late 1100s this pueblo contained more than 600 large rooms around a plaza, with 3 great kivas. Together with the smaller pueblos nearby, the population of the area is estimated to have been between 4,000 and 5,000.

In addition to canals channeling rainwater to their extensive fields, the Chacoan Anasazi built a vast road network. Hundreds of miles of roads, in some places as much as 30 feet wide, radiated out from Chaco. The Chacoans also made use of what appear to be solstice markers, perhaps to help them determine the most advantageous time to perform particular ceremonies. Chaco Canyon came to an end as an Anasazi cultural center in the mid-1100s when its people left the area. An extensive drought during that period is the most likely reason, but they may also have looked for places where game was more plentiful.

Eight pueblos at Chaco Canyon can be reached by car. The others require hiking a few miles. There is a visitor center with a museum 1.5 miles from the southern entrance. The park is open year-round from 8 A.M. to 5 P.M. and to 6 P.M. between Memorial Day and Labor Day. No food, gasoline, or lodging is available in the park or the area around it. Camping is permitted in the sixty-eight-site campground on a first-come, first-served basis. Drinking water can be obtained at the visitor center.

For more information, write to Superintendent, Chaco Culture National Historic Park, Star Route 4, Box 6500, Bloomfield, NM 87413, or telephone 505-786-7014.

13. Gila Cliff Dwellings National Monument

Gila Cliff Dwellings National Monument is located in west-central New Mexico. State Highway 15 leads to it from Silver City, 45 miles south of the monument. State Highway 15 is narrow and winding, and one should allow about two hours to cover the distance. A somewhat longer route using State Highway 35 is recommended for larger vehicles. It branches off State Highway 152 at San Lorenzo (some 20 miles east of Silver City) and then joins State Highway 15 about 19 miles south of the monument.

The main features of the monument are around 40 rooms constructed in several deeply recessed caves in the face of a cliff about 150 feet above the floor of a canyon. These rooms were built by the Mogollon people during the late 1200s. Until then, these canyon dwellers had lived in pit houses and grew the usual crops along the banks of the Gila River, supplementing them with small animals and wild plants. Perhaps they learned masonry from contact with the Ancestral Puebloans (Anasazi). The Gila Cliff Mogollon lived in their cliff village for only about two generations, abandoning it in the early 1300s.

The visitor center is open from 8 A.M. to 5 P.M. during the summer, and from 8 A.M. to 4 P.M. during the rest of the year except for December 25 and January 1. A one-mile loop self-guided trail through the ruins is available. Other sites may be visited only on guided tours. Campgrounds and picnic areas can be found in nearby Gila National Forest. For more information, write to Park Ranger, Gila Cliff Dwellings National Monument, Route 11, Box 100, Silver City, NM 88061, or telephone 505-536-9461.

14. Pecos National Historical Park

Pecos National Historical Park is located off Interstate 25 about 25 miles southeast of Santa Fe and 2 miles south of the village of Pecos.

The park features the ruins of two mission churches built by Franciscans in the seventeenth and eighteenth centuries as well as the ruins of one of the largest pueblos in the Southwest. Construction of some two dozen villages, including one where the Pecos pueblo stands today, began early in the thirteenth century after Ancestral Puebloan (Anasazi) people moved into the Pecos Valley from the northwest and joined the local population. By the fifteenth century, work had begun on a multistoried 700-room fortress that eventually sheltered 2,000 people and greatly impressed members of Coronado's expedition when they came into the area in 1541. The skillful inhabitants of the pueblo engaged in very active trading of pottery, cotton blankets, turquoise, and many additional items with other Pueblos and also Plains Indians, from whom they obtained buffalo hides, antelope and deer skins, meat, tallow, and salt. In the late sixteenth century the pueblo began a slow decline. It was not until 1838 that the last 17 to 20 occupants left the village, joining the people at Jemez Pueblo, their Towa-speaking relatives.

The park is open year-round from 8 A.M. to 5 P.M. The visitor center includes a museum and a bookstore. The ruins are accessible by a 1.3-mile self-guided trail. For more information, write to Superintendent, Pecos National Historical Park, P.O. Box 418, Pecos, NM 87552-0418, or telephone 505-757-6414 (505-757-6032 for visitor center).

15. Petroglyph National Monument

Petroglyph National Monument is located north of Interstate 40 in the northwestern part of Albuquerque west of the Rio Grande. It was established in 1990 to protect and preserve a very large collection of Native American rock art. As of this writing it is still being developed.

Most of the approximately 17,000 petroglyphs (carvings in rock) found on the long West Mesa lava escarpment were incised or pecked into the rock by Pueblo people between 1300 and 1650, but some are as much as 3,000 years old. The oldest petroglyphs show abstract patterns, and the later ones represent human figures and faces (kachina masks?), masked serpent and star beings, insects, reptiles, birds, and other animals. The exact function of these petroglyphs is not known, but it is assumed that at least some of them were created for ceremonial purposes.

For information, write to Superintendent, Petroglyph National Monument, 4735 Unser Blvd. NW, Albuquerque, NM 87120, or telephone 505-839-4429.

Utah

16. Hovenweep National Monument

Hovenweep, meaning "deserted valley" in the Ute language, is located on the extensive Cajon Mesa, which stretches across the Great Sage Plain in southeastern Utah and southwestern Colorado. The monument's ranger station is located about 43 miles west of Cortez, Colorado, and is accessible by way of State Highway 262 in Utah and U.S. Highway 666 from Colorado.

Although the architectural remains at Hovenweep are of communities dating primarily from the thirteenth century, the area was first inhabited several centuries earlier—probably around the year 500. The population of the Hovenweep area is believed to have reached its peak between about 1150 and 1300.

The pueblos of Hovenweep National Monument belong to the prehistoric culture of the Ancestral Puebloans (Anasazi). At first, the structures were relatively small, housing probably not many more than members of one extended family. But the people who inhabited them were accomplished builders and later erected multistoried dwellings.

The monument consists of six clusters of archaeological sites. Two are in Utah, four in Colorado. The ruins closest to the headquarters are the largest and best preserved. They are referred to as the Square Tower Ruins and include Hovenweep Castle, Hovenweep House, and Twin Towers. They are easily reachable by foot trails. The other five ruin clusters are accessible by driving several miles on roads that are unpaved and at times require a four-wheel-drive vehicle. All require a short hiking distance.

Analysis of the pollen recovered from some of the ruins reveals that the people who lived here cultivated corn, beans, squash, and cotton. They supplemented their diet with plants and animals from the wild and may have kept domesticated turkeys. Their pueblos included a variety of specialized structures including kivas, towers, rooms, granaries, water-retaining dams, and water reservoirs. Hovenweep inhabitants fashioned stone and bone tools, ceramic objects, and jewelry. They made clothing from fur, feathers, and cotton.

Occupancy of the Hovenweep pueblos ended during the last quarter of the thirteenth century. One reason is thought to have been an extended drought that affected much of the Southwest, lowering the ground-water level. The population began to move south, and there is general agreement among archaeologists that these people were among the ancestors of the modern Pueblo peoples living in Arizona and New Mexico.

The trails near the ranger station at Square Tower are open from 8 A.M. to 4:30 P.M. year-round, but the road may be impassable during and just after bad weather. The ranger station is open when rangers are not out on patrol. Motel accommodations are available in Bluff and Blanding, Utah, and in Cortez, Colorado. For more information, write to Superintendent, Hovenweep National Monument, McElmo Route, Cortez, CO 81321, or telephone Mesa Verde National Park at 970-529-4461.

APPENDIX A
EXHIBITS RELATING TO
NATIVE AMERICANS
OF THE SOUTHWEST

Anyone interested in learning more about the American Indian cultures of the Southwest will find that many museums, national parks and monuments, state parks, and historic sites maintain exhibits relating to the lives of both prehistoric and present-day Native American peoples. The following information was compiled on the basis of returned questionnaires from a mailing based on the 24th edition (1993) of *The Official Museum Directory,* and has been edited using the 25th edition of the directory (1994).

In order to make it easy to locate museums and visitor centers, the Southwest culture area has been divided into seventeen sections, in part determined by the location of the interstate highway system. The sections are listed below in the following order: Colorado, New Mexico (northeast, southeast, southwest, northwest, Santa Fe and Taos area, and Albuquerque), Texas, Utah, Arizona (northeast, southeast, Tucson area, southwest, Phoenix area, Flagstaff area, and northwest), and Nevada. The map shows these subdivisions. (A few museums outside the Southwest culture area have been included, especially those in central Colorado.)

The name of each museum or visitor center is followed by mailing address, telephone number, and location; times when open; admission charge; the nature of the collections or exhibits concerned with Native Americans of the Southwest, including the availability of libraries and museum shops. Visitors should keep in mind that the times such places are open may change, as may the admission charge. Information concerning accommodations is included in the few instances where such possibilities exist.

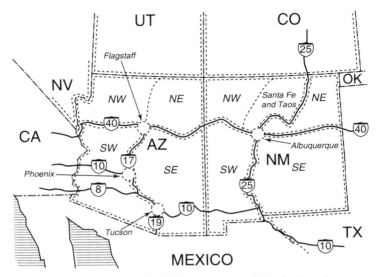

The seventeen geographical subdivisions into which the list of museums has been divided

Colorado

Cortez C.U. (University of Colorado) Center

25 N. Market St., Cortez, CO 81321; 970-565-1151. In downtown Cortez on U.S. 160 near U.S. 666; May–Sept Mo–Sa 10–9, Oct–Apr Mo–Fr 10–5, Sa 11–5; donations only; archaeological, ethnographic, arts and crafts, and photo exh; special programs; gift shop.

Crow Canyon Archaeological Center

23390 County Rd. K, Cortez, CO 81321; 970-565-8975. 4 mi from Cortez; adult research programs (excavation, ethnobotany), Native American cultural explorations, teachers' workshops, high school field school, Southwest seminars, and other programs throughout the yr; housing accom.

Anasazi Heritage Center

27501 Hwy 184, Dolores, CO 81323; 970-882-4811. On SR 184, 10 mi N of Cortez and 3 mi W of Dolores; Mar–Oct 9–5, Nov–Feb 9–4 daily exc Thanksgiving, Dec 25, and Jan 1; free; archaeological, arts and crafts, and photo exh; 2 late Anasazi sites nearby open 8–5 daily.

Mesa Verde National Park Museum

Mesa Verde National Park, P.O. Box 8, Mesa Verde, CO 81330, 970-529-4475. Park entrance approx midway betw Cortez and Mancos off U.S. 160, park HQ 21 mi from entrance; Sept–May 8–5, June–Aug 8–6:30 daily; $5 per car; archaeological and ethnographic exh; dioramas; lib; 3 major cliff dwellings in the park, incl the largest cliff dwelling in North America; campsites; for accom call 970-529-4421 (summer only).

Southern Ute Indian Cultural Center

P.O. Box 737, Ignacio, CO 81137; 970-563-9583. 25 mi SE of Durango, 1 mi N of Ignacio on SR 172; May–Oct Mo–Fr 10–6, Sa–Su 10–3, Nov–Apr Mo–Fr 11–6, Sa 10–3; $1; archaeological, ethnographic, arts and crafts, and photo exh; mus shop.

Telluride Historical Museum

P.O. Box 1597, Telluride, CO 81435; 970-728-3344. Corner of Fir and Gregory in Telluride, approx 50 mi N of Durango, on SR 145. May–Oct 10–5 daily, Nov–Apr Mo–Fr 12–5; $4, sr cit $3, chld $.50; archaeological and arts and crafts exh; lib.

Rimrock Historical Museum of West Montrose County

P.O. Box 305, Nucla, CO 81424; 970-864-7837. N of Main St. in town park of Naturita on SR 141; June 1–Labor Day Tu–Sa 2–5; no adm ch, donations accepted; archaeological, arts and crafts, and photo exh.

University of Colorado Museum

Campus Box 218, Boulder, CO 80309-0218; 303-492-6892. 15th St. and Broadway, near University Memorial Center in Boulder; Mo–Fr 9–5, Sa 9–4, Su 10–4, exc univ hol; free; archaeological, ethnographic, arts and crafts exh.

Denver Art Museum

100 W. 14th Avenue Pkwy., Denver, CO 80204; 303-640-2755. In downtown Denver; Tu–Sa 10–5, Su 12–5, exc major hol; $3.50, students and sr cit $1.50, under 5 free; archaeological, ethnographic, arts and crafts, and photo exh; lib.

Denver Museum of Natural History

2001 Colorado Blvd., Denver, CO 80205-5798; 303-322-7009. In City Park, 3 mi from downtown Denver, 2 mi from I-70; 9–5 daily exc Dec 25; $4.50, chld and sr cit $2.50; archaeological, ethnographic, photo, and arts and crafts exh; lib; mus shop.

State Historical Society of Colorado Museum

1300 Broadway, Denver, CO 80203; 303-866-3682. In downtown Denver; Mo–Sa 10–4:30, Su 12–4:30; $3, sr cit $2.50, chld 1.50; archaeological, ethnographic, arts and crafts, and photo exh; lib; mus shop.

Manitou Cliff Dwellings Museum

P.O. Box 272, Manitou Springs, CO 80829; 719-685-5242. 5 mi W of Colorado Springs on U.S. 24; June–Aug 9–8, Mar–May and Sept–Nov 9–5 daily; $4, chld $2; archaeological exh; mus shop.

El Pueblo Museum

324 W. 1st St., Pueblo, CO 81003; 719-583-0453. Corner of W. 1st St. and Grand Ave., 3 blocks from I-25, Exit 98B; Tu–Sa 10–3; $2.50, chld and sr cit $1; archaeological, ethnographic, and photo exh; gift shop.

Rocky Ford Historical Museum

P.O. Box 835, Rocky Ford, CO 81067; 719-254-6737. On U.S. 50 approx 50 mi E of Pueblo; mid-May to mid-Sept Tu–Sa 11–4, mid-Sept to mid-May Fr–Sa 1–4; free; archaeological exh.

Koshare Indian Museum

P.O. Box 580, La Junta, CO 81050; 719-384-4411. 115 W. 18th St., La Junta, on U.S. 50 close to junction with U.S. 350; June–Aug Mo–Sa 9–5, Su 12:30–5, Sept–May Tu–Su 12:30–4:30; $2, chld and sr cit $1; archaeological, ethnographic, and arts and crafts exh; lib; mus shop.

Arthur Roy Mitchell Memorial Museum of Western Art

P.O. Box 95, Trinidad, CO 81082; 719-846-4224. 150 E. Main St. in Trinidad on I-25; Apr–Sept Mo–Sa 10–4; no adm ch, donations accepted; ethnographic and arts and crafts exh.

Fort Francisco Museum

P.O. Box 428, La Veta, CO 81055. Main St. of La Veta on SR 12, approx 5 mi S of U.S. 160. Mem Day–Labor Day 9–5 daily; $2, chld $.75; local archaeological exh.

Adams State College Museums

208 Edgemont Blvd., Alamosa, CO 81102; 719-589-7011. Richardson Hall on Adams State College campus, off U.S. 160; Mo–Fr 1–5 exc nat hol; free; archaeological, ethnographic, and cult hist exh.

Saguache County Museum

P.O. Box 569, Saguache, CO 81149; 719-655-2557. Near the junction of U.S. 285 and SR 114 on U.S. 285; Mem Day–Labor Day 10–5 daily; $2, under 12 $.50; archaeological, ethnographic, and photo exh.

Salida Museum

406 1/2 W. Rainbow Blvd., Salida, CO 81201; 719-539-2311. Next to Salida hot springs pool, directly behind the Chamber of Commerce on U.S. 50; Mem Day–Labor Day Th–Su 12–7; no adm ch, donations accepted; archaeological, ethnographic, arts and crafts, and photo exh.

New Mexico (Northeast)

Tucumcari Historical Museum

416 S. Adams St., Tucumcari, NM 88401; 505-461-4201. 4 blocks from U.S. 66 or U.S. 54, 1 block from SR 18; summer Mo–Sa 9–6 and Su 1–6, winter (Sept 2–June 2) Tu–Sa 9–5 and Su 1–5; $2, chld $.50; archaeological exh.

New Mexico (Southeast)

Fort Sumner State Monument

P.O. Box 356, Fort Sumner, NM 88119-0356; 505-355-2573. 3 mi E of Fort Sumner and 3 mi S off U.S. 60/84 on Billy the Kid Road; May to mid-Sept Th–Su 9:30–5:30, mid-Sept through Apr Th–Su 8:30–4:30 exc winter hol; $1, under 10 free; archaeological and photo exh.

Roswell Museum and Art Center

100 W. 11th St., Roswell, NM 88201; 505-624-6744. In Roswell, 100 W. 11th St. (corner of Main St.); Mo–Sa 9–5, Su and hol 1–5, exc Thanksgiving, Dec 25, and Jan 1; free; archaeological, ethnographic, arts and crafts, and photo exh; lib.

Artesia Historical Museum and Art Center

505 W. Richardson Ave., Artesia, NM 88210; 505-748-2390. Tu–Sa 10–12 and 1–5 exc nat hol; free; archaeological, ethnographic, arts and crafts, and photo exh; lib.

Carlsbad Museum and Art Center

418 W. Fox St., Carlsbad, NM 88220; 505-887-0276. Mo–Sa 10–6; no adm ch, donations accepted; archaeological and arts and crafts exh; mus shop.

Mescalero Apache Cultural Center

P.O. Box 176, Mescalero, NM 88340; 505-671-4494, ext 254. Mescalero Apache Reservation, Chiricahua Plaza, off U.S. 70; Mo–Fr 8–4:30; free; archaeological, ethnographic, and photo exh.

Tularosa Basin Historical Society Museum

Box 518, Alamogordo, NM 88310; 505-437-4760. 1301 N. White Sands Blvd., Alamogordo; Mo–Sa 10–4, Su 1–4, closed on nat hol; free; archaeological and photo exh.

Geronimo Springs Museum

211 Main St., Truth or Consequences, NM 87901; 505-894-6600. Via exits from I-25 to the center of Truth or Consequences; Mo–Sa 9–5; $2, chld $1; archaeological, ethnographic, and photo exh.

Salinas Pueblo Missions National Monument Visitor Center

P.O. Box 496, Mountainair, NM 87036-0496; 505-847-2585. Corner of Ripley St. and U.S. 60 in Mountainair; 9–5 daily exc Dec 25 and Jan 1; free; archaeological exh; one museum at Gran Quirira Unit, the other at Quarai Unit, about 35 mi apart.

New Mexico (Southwest)

New Mexico State University Museum

P.O. Box 3564, Las Cruces, NM 88003-0001; 505-646-3739. Kent Hall on campus of NMSU, corner of University Ave. at Solano Dr.; Tu–Sa 10–4, Su 1–4, exc nat hol; free; archaeological, ethnographic, arts and crafts, and photo exh; lib; mus shop.

Deming Luna Mimbres Museum

301 S. Silver Ave., Deming, NM 88030; 505-546-2382. Exit from I-10 at Deming, Motel Drive to stoplight at Gold Ave, 2 blocks S, 1 block E; Mo–Sa 9–4, Su 1:30–4, exc Thanksgiving and Dec 25; free; archaeological, ethnographic, arts and crafts, and photo exh; books.

Western New Mexico University Museum

P.O. Box 680, Silver City, NM 88602; 505-538-6386. Fleming Hall, 10th St., WNMU campus; Mo–Fr 9–4:30, Sa and Su 10–4, exc univ hol; free; archaeological and arts and crafts exh; books.

Gila Cliff Dwellings National Monument Visitor Center

Rt 11, Box 100, Silver City, NM 88061; 505-536-9461. 45 mi N of Silver City on SR 15; 8–4 daily, extended hours in summer; free; archaeological, ethnographic, and arts and crafts exh; gift shop.

A:Shiwi A:Wan Museum and Heritage Center

P.O. Box 1009, Zuni, NM 87327; 505-782-4403. SR 53, Building 1222, E of Tribal Building behind new Zuni Pueblo Arts and Crafts Building; Mo–Fr 8–4; free; photo exh.

El Morro National Monument

El Morro National Monument, Rt 2, Box 43, Ramah, NM 87321-9603; 505-783-4226. 57 mi SE of Gallup via SR 602 and 53; 45 mi SW of Grants via SR 53; 8–7 daily Mem Day–Labor Day, otherwise 8–5 daily exc Dec 25; $2 per person, $4 per carload; archaeological, ethnographic, arts and crafts, and photo exh; gift shop.

El Malpais National Monument Visitor Center

P.O. Box 939, Grants, NM 87020; 505-285-4641. 620 East Santa Fe Ave., Grants, NM (the 178 sq mi area constituting the national monument is S of Grants; the Zuni-Acoma Trail is available for hiking [7 1/2 mi one way, trailhead 18 mi S of I-40]); summer 8–5 daily, winter Mo–Sa 8–4:30 exc Thanksgiving, Dec 25, and Jan 1; free; archaeological, ethnographic, and photo exh.

New Mexico (Northwest)

Red Rock Museum

P.O. Box 328, Church Rock, NM 87311; 505-863-1337. Exit 26 from I-40 E of Gallup, 2 mi E on frontage rd. (signs for Red Rock State Park); summer 8–7 daily, otherwise Mo–Fr 8:30–4:30; $1, chld $.50; archaeological, ethnographic, arts and crafts, and photo exh; gift shop; Red Rock State Park has campgrounds and other facilities.

Farmington Museum

302 N. Orchard Ave., Farmington, NM 87401; 505-599-1179. 3 blocks N of Main St. on the NW corner of Orchard and LaPlata; Tu–Fr 12–5, Sa 10–5; free; arts and crafts, ethnographic, and photo exh.

Aztec Museum and Pioneer Village

125 N. Main St., Aztec, NM 87410; 505-334-9829. On SR 544, just off U.S. 550; summer Mo–Sa 9–5, winter Mo–Sa 10–4; $1; archaeological, ethnographic, arts and crafts, and photo exh; lib.

Aztec Ruins National Monument Visitor Center

P.O. Box 640, Aztec, NM 87410-0640; 505-334-6174. 3/4 mi N of intersection of U.S. 550 and Ruins Rd. in Aztec; Mem Day–Labor Day 8–6 daily, otherwise 8–5 exc Thanksgiving, Dec 25 and Jan 1; $2; archaeological and ethnographic exh; bookshop.

San Juan County
Archaeological Research Center

P.O. Box 215, Bloomfield, NM 87413; 505-632-2013. On U.S. 64, 2 mi W of Bloomfield; 9–5 daily; $2, sr cit $1.50, chld $1; archaeological, ethnographic, arts and crafts, and photo exh; lib; Salmon pueblo ruin (abandoned in the late 1200s) nearby.

Chaco Culture National Historical Park Visitor Center

Star Rte 4, Box 6500, Bloomfield, NM 87413; 505-786-7014. Turn off SR 44 at Nageezi, then via San Juan County Rd. 7900 for 11 mi to SR 57—vis cent 15 mi ahead; Labor Day–Mem Day 8–5 daily, otherwise 8–6 daily exc Dec 25 and Jan 1; adm ch $4 for park; archaeological and ethnographic exh.

New Mexico (Santa Fe and Taos Area)

Pecos National Historical Park, E. E. Fogelson Visitor Center

P.O. Box 418, Pecos, NM 87552-0418; 505-757-6032. 25 mi SE of Santa Fe, off I-25 on SR 63, 2 mi S of Pecos; 8–5 daily exc Dec 25; $2; archaeological, ethnographic, and photo exh; lib.

Museum of Indian Arts and Culture (Museum of New Mexico)

P.O. Box 2087, Santa Fe, NM 87504-2087; 505-827-6344. 710 Camino Lejo, across the parking area from the Mus of International Folk Art; 10–5 daily exc Mo in Jan and Feb and on nat hol; $4, under 16 free; archaeological, ethnographic, arts and crafts, and photo exh; lib.

Wheelwright Museum of the American Indian

P.O. Box 5153, Santa Fe, NM 87502; 505-982-4636. 704 Camino Lejo, Santa Fe; Mo–Sa 10–5, Su 1–5; free; archaeological, ethnographic, arts and crafts, and photo exh; books; mus houses Case Trading Post.

The Palace of the Governors

P.O. Box 2087, Santa Fe, NM 87504; 505-827-6474. N side of Plaza on Palace Ave.; Jan–Feb Tu–Su 10–5, otherwise 10–5 daily; 3-day 4-

museum pass $5, under 17 free; ethnographic, arts and crafts, and photo exh; books; Portal Native American Vendor Program.

Institute of American
Indian Arts Museum

Box 20007, Santa Fe, NM 87501; 505-988-6281. 108 Cathedral Place, Santa Fe; Mar–Dec Mo–Sa 10–5, Su 12–5, Jan–Feb Tu–Su 10–5; $4, students and sr cit $2, under 12 free; contemp Native Amer and Alaskan art exh.

National Park Service,
Southwest Region

P.O. Box 728, Santa Fe, NM 87504-0728. 1100 Old Santa Fe Trail, Santa Fe; Mo–Fr 8–4:30; free; archaeological, ethnographic, arts and crafts, and photo exh; books.

Bandelier National Monument

Bandelier National Monument, HCR 1, Box 1, Suite 15, Los Alamos, NM 87544-9701; 505-672-3861. 8 mi from White Rock on SR 4, 48 mi W of Santa Fe; summer 8–6, winter 8–4:30 daily; $5 per vehicle; archaeological, ethnographic, arts and crafts, and photo exh; gift shop.

Los Alamos County
Historical Museum

P.O. Box 43, Los Alamos, NM 87544; 505-662-6272. Adjacent to Fuller Lodge Cultural Center off Central Ave., 1921 Juniper St., Los Alamos; summer Mo–Sa 9:30–4:30, Su 11–5, winter Mo–Sa 10–4, Su 1–4, exc nat hol; free; archaeological, ethnographic, arts and crafts, and photo exh; lib; mus shop.

Florence Hawley Ellis
Museum of Anthropology

Ghost Ranch Conference Center, HC 77, Box 11, Abiquiu, NM 87510-9601; 505-685-4333. On U.S. 84; Jan–Nov Tu–Sa 9–12 and 1–5, Su 1–5; free; archaeological, ethnographic, arts and crafts exh; lib; gift shop.

Governor Bent Museum

P.O. Box 153, Taos, NM 87571; 505-758-2376. 117 Bent St., 1 block N of Plaza, in Taos; summer 9–5 daily, winter 10–4 daily; $1, chld 8–15 $.50; arts and crafts and photo exh; books; gift shop.

Taos Pueblo

Taos Pueblo Governor's Office, P.O. Box 1846, Taos, NM 87571; 505-758-1028. 2 mi N of Taos on N. Pueblo Rd.; summer 8–5, winter 9–4 daily; parking $5 per car; photo; gift shop.

Millicent Rogers Museum

P.O. Box A, Taos, NM 87571; 505-758-2462. 4 mi N of Taos Plaza near U.S. 64 at 1504 Millicent Rogers Rd.; 9–5 daily; $6 family, $4 adults, $3 sr cit and students; archaeological, ethnographic, arts and crafts, and photo exh; books.

Philmont Museum

Philmont Scout Ranch, Cimarron, NM 87714; 505-376-2281, ext 46. May–Sept 8–5 daily, otherwise Mo–Fr 8–5; $1 per car, $2 on weekends; archaeological, ethnographic, arts and crafts, and photo exh; books.

New Mexico (Albuquerque)

Petroglyph National Monument
Visitor Center

4735 Unser Blvd. NW, Albuquerque, NM 87120; 505-839-4429. 8–5 daily exc Thanksgiving, Dec 25, and Jan 1; $1 per car, $2 on weekends; over 15,000 Puebloan petroglyphs.

Indian Pueblo Cultural
Center Museum

2401 12th St. NW, Albuquerque, NM 87102; 505-843-7270. 1 block N of I-40 on the corner of 12th St. and Menaul Blvd.; 9–5:30 daily exc Thanksgiving, Dec 25, Jan 1, and Jan 6; $2.50, sr cit $1.50, students and chld $1; archaeological, ethnographic, arts and crafts, and photo exh.

Texas

Chamizal National Memorial

800 S. San Marcial, El Paso, TX 79905; 915-534-6668. Corner of San Marcial and Paisano, adjacent to the international boundary, via Exit 22B from I-10 onto U.S. 54 for approx 1 mi S; May–Oct 10–7 and Nov–Apr 8–5 daily exc Thanksgiving, Dec 25, and Jan 1; free; ethnographic and photo exh; bookstore.

Big Bend National Park Visitor Center

P.O. Box 129, Big Bend National Park, TX 79834; 915-477-2251. Park HQ approx 100 mi S of Marathon on U.S. 385 or approx 108 mi S of Alpine on SR 118; 8–6 daily; $5 per car; ethnographic exh; campsites; for accom call 915-477-2291.

Utah

Dan O'Laurie Museum

118 E. Center, Moab, UT 84532; 801-259-7985. On U.S. 191 in Moab; summer 1–5 and 7–9 daily, winter Mo–Th 3–5 and 7–9, Fr–Sa 1–5 and 7–9, exc nat hol; no adm ch, donations accepted; archaeological exh.

Canyonlands National Park Visitor Centers

125 W. 200 South, Moab, UT 84532; 801-259-7164. To Island in the Sky Vis Cent on SR 313 from U.S. 191, approx 35 mi SW of Moab; to Needles Vis Cent on SR 211 from U.S. 191, approx 50 mi NW of Monticello; daily; $4 per car; archaeological (Anasazi), ethnographic, and photo exh; campsites.

Edge of the Cedars State Park Museum

P.O. Box 788, Blanding, UT 84511-0788; 801-678-2238. NW of Blanding at 660 W. 400 North; follow signs from U.S. 191 from the center of Blanding for 1 mi; mid-Sept to mid-May 9–5 and mid-May to mid-Sept 9–6 daily exc nat hol; $1.50, chld 6–15 $1; archaeological (Anasazi) and ethnographic (Navajo, Ute) exh; lib; mus shop; also: Edge of the Cedars Indian ruin (a small Anasazi village occupied approx A.D. 750–1220).

Natural Bridges National Monument Visitor Center

P.O. Box 1, Lake Powell, UT 84533; 801-259-5174. Approx 40 mi W of Blanding, 4 mi N on SR 275 from SR 95; summer 7–6, winter 9–4:30 daily; $4 per car; archaeological and photo exh.

Anasazi Indian Village State Park

P.O. Box 1329, Boulder, UT 84716-1329; 801-335-7308. On Canyon Rd. in Boulder off SR 12; summer 8–6, otherwise 9–5 daily; $1.50, chld $1, small chld and sr cit free; archaeological and photo exh; diorama of original village.

Bryce Canyon National Park Visitor Center

Bryce Canyon, UT 84717; 801-834-5322. Approx 25 mi SE of Panguitch; from U.S. 89 take SR 12 and then SR 63 to enter the park; summer 8–8, otherwise 8–4:30 daily exc hol; $5 per car; local area archaeological and photo exh; for camping and accom call 801-586-7686.

Zion National Park Visitor Centers

Springdale, UT 84767-1099; 801-772-3256. Main center at park HQ on SR 9, 1 mi N of Springdale; Kolob Canyons center 18 mi S of Cedar City off I-15; summer 8–8 and winter 8–5 daily; $5 per car or $3 per person; archaeological, ethnographic, arts and crafts, and photo exh; lib; for camping and accom call 800-869-6635.

Arizona (Northeast)

Canyon de Chelly National Monument

P.O. Box 588, Chinle, AZ 86503; 520-674-5500. Intersection of Navajo Routes 7 and 64, 3 mi E of Chinle; May–Oct 8–6 daily, otherwise 8–5 daily; free; archaeological, ethnographic, arts and crafts, and photo exh; bookstore.

Hubbell Trading Post National Historic Site

P.O. Box 150, Ganado, AZ 86505; 520-755-3475. 1 mi W of Ganado, approx 25 mi W of Window Rock on SR 264; Oct–Apr 8–5 daily, May–Sept 8–6 daily exc Thanksgiving, Dec 25, and Jan 1; free; archaeological, ethnographic, arts and crafts, and photo exh; books; gift shop.

Navajo Nation Museum

P.O. Box 9000, Window Rock, AZ 86515; 520-871-6673. On SR 264 in Window Rock; Mo–Fr 9–4:45 exc nat and tribal hol; no adm ch, donations accepted; archaeological, ethnographic, and photo exh.

Homolovi Ruins State Park

HC 63, Box 5, Winslow, AZ 86047; 520-289-4106. 1 mi N of I-40, Exit 257, on SR 87 (Second Mesa Rd.), approx 3 mi NE of Winslow; 8–5 daily exc Dec 25; $3 per car; archaeological and ethnographic exh; gift shop.

Arizona (Southeast)

Pine-Strawberry Museum

P.O. Box 564, Pine, AZ 85544; 520-476-3223. On SR 87, on the left side of Community Center in Pine; May–Oct Fr–Sa 10–4, Su 1–4; free; archaeological and photo exh; books.

White Mountain Apache Cultural Center

P.O. Box 507, Fort Apache, AZ 85926; 520-338-4625. On SR 73; Mo–Fr 8–5; free; archaeological, ethnographic, arts and crafts, and photo exh.

Tonto National Monument

HC O2, Box 4602, Roosevelt, AZ 85545; 520-467-2241. On SR 88, S of Theodore Roosevelt Lake, 30 mi NW of Globe, 55 mi S of Payson; museum 8–5 daily, ruins trail 8–4 daily; mus free, ruins $4 per car; archaeological and photo exh; books.

Besh-Ba-Gowah Archaeological Park

City of Globe, 150 N. Pine St., Globe, AZ 85501; 520-425-0320. On Jess Hayes Rd. 2 mi S of downtown Globe, adjacent to the Globe Community Center; 8–5 daily exc Thanksgiving, Dec 25, and Jan 1; $2, 12 and under free; archaeological, ethnographic, and photo exh; gift shop.

Gila County Historical Museum

P.O. Box 2891, Globe, AZ 88501; 520-425-7385. 1330 N. Broad St., Globe, on U.S. 60 and 70; Mo–Fr 10–4; free; basketry and photo exh.

Eastern Arizona College Museum of Anthropology

Eastern Arizona College, Thatcher, AZ 85552-0769; 520-428-8310. Eastern Arizona College campus on College Ave., 1/2 block S of U.S. 70, in Thatcher; 9–12 and 1–4 weekdays during acad yr; free; archaeological and ethnographic exh; books.

Graham County Historical Society

P.O. Box 323, Safford, AZ 85552; 520-348-3212. 808 8th Ave., Safford; Mo and Tu 1–5 exc nat hol; archaeological and arts and crafts exh.

Fort Bowie National Historic Site

P.O. Box 158, Bowie, AZ 85605; 520-847-2500. 13 mi S of Bowie on Apache Pass Rd.; 8–5 daily exc Dec 25; free; ethnographic, arts and crafts, and photo exh.

Museum of the Southwest

1500 N. Circle I Rd., Willcox, AZ 85643; 520-384-2272. I-10 Exit 340; Mo–Sa 9–5, Su 1–5; free; archaeological, ethnographic, arts and crafts, and photo exh; books.

Chiricahua National Monument

Dos Cabezas Rt., Box 6500, Willcox, AZ 85643; 520-824-3560. 38 mi SE of Willcox on SR 186; 8–5 daily exc Dec 25; $4 per vehicle; ethnographic exh; bookstore.

The Amerind Foundation

P.O. Box 400, Dragoon, AZ 85609; 520-586-3666. 65 mi E of Tucson off I-10 via Exit 318 (Dragoon Rd.) for 1 mi E to the Amerind Foundation turnoff, turn left at sign; Sept–May 10–4 daily, June–Aug 10–4 We–Su; $3, sr cit and chld 12–18 $2; archaeological, ethnographic, and photo exh.

Coronado National Monument

R.R. 1, Box 126 or 4101 E. Montezuma Canyon Rd., Hereford, AZ 85615; 520-366-5515. 15 mi S of Sierra Vista or 25 mi W of Bisbee on SR 92 to Coronado Mem Rd., then 5 mi up Montezuma Canyon; 8–5 daily; free; arts and crafts, books, and other exh.

Tumacacori National Historical Park

P.O. Box 67, Tumacacori, AZ 85640; 520-398-2341. Exit 29 off I-19, 45 mi S of Tucson; 8–5 daily exc Thanksgiving and Dec 25; $2 over 16 and under 62; archaeological, ethnographic, arts and crafts, and photo exh.

Pinal County Historical Society Museum

P.O. Box 851, Florence, AZ 85237; 520-868-4382. 715 S. Main St., Florence; Apr–Nov 12–4 We–Su, Dec–Mar 11–4 We–Su, closed July 15–Sept 1; no adm ch, donations accepted; ethnographic, arts and crafts, and photo exh; books.

Casa Grande Ruins National Monument

1100 Ruins Dr., Coolidge, AZ 85228; 520-723-3172. Entrance off SR 87/287, N end of Coolidge; 8–5 daily exc Dec 25; $2, under 16 free; archaeological and ethnographic exh.

Casa Grande History Museum

110 W. Florence Blvd., Casa Grande, AZ 85222; 520-836-2223. Exit 194 off I-10 onto Florence Blvd., 4 mi W into Casa Grande; Sept 15–June 15 Tu–Su 1–5; $1, chld free; archaeological, ethnographic, arts and crafts, and photo exh; books.

Arizona (Tucson Area)

Catalina State Park

P.O. Box 36986, Tucson, AZ 85740; 520-628-5798. Milepost 81 on N. Oracle Rd. NW of Tucson; 7 A.M.–10 P.M. daily; $3 per car; archaeological exh; self-guided trail through a Hohokam village site; camping facilities.

Tohono Chul Park

7366 N. Paseo del Norte, Tucson, AZ 85704; 520-742-6455. In Tucson at first stoplight on Ina Rd. W of Oracle Rd.; grounds 7 to sunset, buildings 9:30–5 Mo–Sa, 11–5 Su, exc July 4; suggested donation $2; arts and crafts exh; lib.

Arizona State Museum

Arizona State Museum, University of Arizona, Tucson, AZ 85721; 520-621-6281. Univ of Arizona campus, just inside the Main Gate at Park Ave. and University Blvd.; Mo–Sa 10–5, Su 12–5; free; archaeological, ethnographic, arts and crafts, and photo exh; lib and gift shop.

Arizona (Southwest)

Tuzigoot National Monument Visitor Center

P.O. Box 68, Clarkdale, AZ 86324; 520-634-5564. Betw Cottonwood and Clarkdale, off Broadway, approx 2 mi E of Clarkdale off U.S. 89A; summer 8–7 and winter 8–5 daily; $2, sr cit free; archaeological exh (ruins of several pueblos occupied approx A.D. 100–1425).

Montezuma Castle National Monument Visitor Center

P.O. Box 219, Camp Verde, AZ 86322; 520-567-3322. 5 mi N of Camp Verde, off I-17; summer 8–7 and winter 8–5 daily; $2, under 18 and sr cit free; archaeological, ethnographic, arts and crafts, and photo exh; bookshop; five-story ruin in a cliff alcove.

Fort Verde State Historic Park

P.O. Box 397, Camp Verde, AZ 86322; 520-567-3275. Off I-17 in Camp Verde at 125 E. Hollamon St.; 8–4:30 daily exc Dec 25; $2, age 12–17 $1, under 12 free; some exh concerning local cultures, mainly as related to the U.S. Army during the Indian wars in the Southwest.

Sharlot Hall Museum

415 W. Gurley St., Prescott, AZ 86301; 520-445-3122. 2 blocks W of Yavapai County Courthouse; May–Oct Mo–Sa 10–5, Su 1–5, Nov–Apr Tu–Sa 10–4, Su 1–5; $2 donation requested; archaeological and ethnographic exh; books.

Bead Museum

140 S. Montezuma St., Prescott, AZ 86303; 520-445-2431. W side of Courthouse Plaza in Prescott; Mo–Sa 9:30–4:30; free; ethnographic exh; books.

Desert Caballeros Western Museum

P.O. Box 1446, Wickenburg, AZ 85358; 520-684-2272. 60 mi NW of Phoenix on the NW corner of intersection of U.S. 90 and 63, at 21 N. Frontier St., center of Wickenburg; Mo–Sa 10–4, Su 1–4, exc major hol; $4, sr cit $3.50; archaeological, arts and crafts, and photo exh; books; gift shop.

Colorado River Indian Tribes Museum

Rt 1, Box 23-B, Parker, AZ 85344; 520-669-9211. 2 mi S of Parker off SR 95, at Second Ave. and Mohave Rd.; Mo–Fr 8–12, 1–5, Sa 10–3, closed Su and hol; free; archaeological, ethnographic, arts and crafts, and photo exh; books.

Quechan Museum

P.O. Box 11352, Yuma, AZ 85366-9352; 619-572-0661. In Yuma, N via 1st St., under I-8, to Fort Yuma Indian Hill; Mo–Fr 8–5, Sa 10–4; $1, under 12 free; arts and crafts shop.

Arizona (Phoenix Area)

Cave Creek Museum

P.O. Box 1, Cave Creek, AZ 85331; 602-488-2764. 6140 Skyline Dr., Cave Creek, AZ, N of Phoenix; We–Su 1–4:30 exc Thanksgiving and Dec 25; free; archaeological, ethnographic, arts and crafts, and photo exh; books.

Phoenix Museum of History

P.O. Box 926, Phoenix, AZ 85001; 602-253-2734. In downtown Phoenix at Fifth and Monroe Sts.; Mo–Sa 10–5, Su 12–5, exc hol; $5, sr cit $3.50, chld $2.50, 6 and under free; archaeological, ethno-graphic, and photo exh; books.

Heard Museum

22 E. Monte Vista Rd., Phoenix, AZ 85004-1480; 602-252-8840. 1 block E of Central Ave. and 3 blocks N of McDowell Rd.; Mo–Sa 10–5, We 10–9, Su 12–5, exc Jan 1, Easter, Mem Day, July 4, Labor

Day, Thanksgiving, and Dec 25; $5, chld 4–12 $2; archaeological, ethnographic, arts and crafts, and photo exh; books; gift shop; nationally acclaimed museum.

Pueblo Grande Museum and Cultural Park

4619 E. Washington St., Phoenix, AZ 85034-1909; 602-495-0901. In downtown Phoenix; Mo–Sa 9–4:45, Su 1–4:45; $.50, under 6 free; archaeological, ethnographic, arts and crafts, and photo exh; ruins on site; books in gift shop.

Arizona State University Museum of Anthropology

P.O. Box 872402, Tempe, AZ 85287-2402; 602-965-6213. On ASU campus, S of the intersection of College and University Dr.; Mo–Fr 8–5; free; archaeological or ethnographic exh.

Mesa Southwest Museum

53 N. MacDonald Rd., Mesa, AZ 85201-7325; 602-644-2169. 1 block N of Main St. at NE corner of First St. and N. MacDonald Rd.; Tu–Sa 10–5, Su 1–5; $4, chld $2; archaeological, ethnographic, arts and crafts, and photo exh; books.

Chandler Museum

P.O. Box 926, Chandler, AZ 85244; 602-786-2842. 178 E. Commonwealth Ave., Chandler; Oct–May 12–4 daily exc hol; free; archaeological and ethnographic exh.

Arizona (Flagstaff Area)

Wupatki National Monument Visitor Center

HC 33 Box 444A, Flagstaff, AZ 86001; 520-679-2365. 35 mi NE of Flagstaff off U.S. 89, approx 20 mi N of Sunset Crater; 8–5 daily exc Dec 25; $4 per car; archaeological, ethnographic, and photo exh; lib; bookshop.

Sunset Crater Volcano National
Monument Visitor Center

Route 3, Box 149, Flagstaff, AZ 86004; 520-556-7042. Approx 15 mi N of Flagstaff on SR 3 off U.S. 89; 8–5 daily exc Dec 25 and Jan 1; $4 per car; archaeological, ethnographic, arts and crafts, and photo exh; bookshop.

Walnut Canyon National Monument

Walnut Canyon Rd., Flagstaff, AZ 86004; 520-526-3367. 7.5 mi E of Flagstaff and 3 mi off I-40; summer 8–6, winter 9–5 daily exc Thanksgiving and Dec 25; $3 per car, $1 per person; archaeological, ethnographic, and photo exh; lib; bookstore.

Museum of Northern Arizona

Route 4, Box 720, Flagstaff, AZ 86001; 520-774-5213. On U.S. 180 in N Flagstaff at 3001 N. Fort Valley Rd.; 9–5 daily; $4, sr cit $3, students 21 and under $2; archaeological, ethnographic, arts and crafts, photo exh; lib; mus shop; nationally acclaimed museum.

Arizona (Northwest)

Pipe Spring National Monument

HC 65, Box 5, Fredonia, AZ 86022; 520-643-7105. 14 mi SW of Fredonia off SR 389; 8–4 daily; $2, chld free; ethnographic exh; small adjoining campground administered by the Paiute tribe.

John Wesley Powell Memorial Museum

P.O. Box 547, Page, AZ 86040; 520-645-9496. Off U.S. 89 at 6 N. Lake Powell Blvd., corner of N. Navajo Dr. in Page; May–Sept Mo–Sa 8–6, Su 10–6; during Oct–Apr call for information; $1, chld $.50; archaeological and arts and crafts exh; lib; museum shop.

Carl Hayden Visitor Center

P.O. Box 1507, Page, AZ 86040; 520-645-8404. U.S. 89 and Lakeshore Dr., Page (near Glen Canyon Dam); summer 7–7 and winter 8:30–5, daily exc Dec 25 and Jan 1; free; archaeological and ethnographic exh.

Tusayan Museum, Grand Canyon National Park

Grand Canyon National Park, P.O. Box 129, Grand Canyon, AZ 86023; 520-638-2305. South rim of Grand Canyon National Park, 3 mi W of east entrance at Desert View, approx 35 mi on SR 64 from Cameron; 8–5 daily exc Dec 25, expanded hours during summer; parking $10 per car; archaeological, ethnographic, arts and crafts, and photo exh; bookshop; excavated Anasazi ruin adjacent to mus.

Mohave Museum of History and Arts

400 W. Beale St., Kingman, AZ 86401; 520-753-3195. Off I-40 in Kingman; Mo–Fr 10–5, Sa–Su 1–5, exc Jan 1, Easter, Mem Day, Labor Day, Thanksgiving, and Dec 25; $2, under 12 free; archaeological, ethnographic, arts and crafts, and photo exh; lib; mus shop.

Nevada

Lost City Museum

P.O. Box 807, Overton, NV 89040; 702-397-2193. 721 S. Moapa Valley Blvd. (SR 169), Overton, approx 12 mi S of I-15 at Interchange 93; 8:30–4:30 daily exc Thanksgiving, Dec 25, and Jan 1; $2; archaeological, ethnographic, arts and crafts, and photo exh; lib; mus shop.

Nevada State Museum and Historical Society

700 Twin Lakes Dr., Las Vegas, NV 89107; 702-486-5205. In Lorenzi Park, Las Vegas, approx 3 mi W of I-15 just off W. Washington Ave.; 9–5 daily exc Thanksgiving, Dec 25, and Jan 1; $2; archaeological and ethnographic exh; lib; mus shop.

Marjorie Barrick Museum of Natural History

4505 S. Maryland Pkwy., Las Vegas, NV 89154-4012; 702-739-3381. Mo–Fr 9–5, Sa 10–2, exc nat hol; free; archaeological exh; mus shop.

Clark County Heritage Museum

1830 S. Boulder Hwy., Henderson, NV 89015; 702-455-7955. In Henderson, approx 11 mi SE of Las Vegas; 9–4 daily exc Thanksgiving and

Dec 25; $1, chld and sr cit $.50; prehist, cultural hist, and ethnographic exh.

Alan Bible Visitor Center—
Lake Mead National Recreation Area

601 Nevada Hwy., Boulder City, NV 89005-2426; 702-293-8906. Intersection of U.S. 93 and SR 166, 2 mi E of Boulder City and approx 20 mi SE of Las Vegas; 8:30–4:30 daily exc Thanksgiving, Dec 25, and Jan 1; free; archaeological exh; lib.

APPENDIX B
SPECIAL EVENTS

Many Native American special events that occur on a more or less regular basis throughout the year in the Southwest are colorful and enjoyable. The list that follows has been compiled from various sources as well as from responses to a questionnaire we sent out. Although it may not be exhaustive, it includes most of the events thousands of interested visitors make a point of attending each year.

In the various pueblos these events take place in the village plazas. There are usually specially designated places from which non-Pueblo people can view the proceedings. Quite frequently ceremonies last several days and some or parts may not be open to the public. Most take place during the summer months (June through August), usually on weekends, but every month of the year a ceremony of some type is scheduled for somewhere in the Southwest.

The Native Americans are very generous people, and as a rule they welcome visitors who are interested in special events open to the public. Unfortunately, visitors do not always conduct themselves appropriately. It cannot be emphasized strongly enough that during tribal ceremonies, many of which are sacred in nature, visitors are expected to be quiet and respectful, just as they would expect others to behave in churches or other places of worship. Furthermore, when visiting the various reservations of the Southwest, it is important to keep in mind that the land belongs to the tribes, visitors are guests, and the privacy of those whose home it is should be respected. For example, visitors should always ask permission before venturing off the main road; otherwise they may drive across or stop in areas that are considered sacred, or at least not suitable for casual visiting (for example, burial places). No one should take photographs or make sketches, sound recordings, films, or videotapes of ceremonies unless permission is obtained from a person who is authorized to give such permission. The same restrictions apply to photographing Native Americans, who may be quite sensitive about such things. In other words, visitors should behave as they would like strangers visiting their own homes or communities to behave.

One more important note: Concerning the dates listed, we caution readers that because exact dates vary from year to year, in many cases the *dates are approximate.* Occasionally some ceremonies are announced only a few days in advance. We strongly recommend that potential visitors check locally as to when and where events are scheduled and whether they are open to the public. We have listed the administrative bodies or persons to contact and their telephone numbers whenever they have been obtainable. Information may also be available from the Arizona Office of Tourism, 1100 West Washington Street, Phoenix, AZ 85007 (800-842-8257 or 602-542-8687); the Arizona Commission of Indian Affairs, 1400 West Washington Street, Suite 300, Phoenix, AZ 85007 (602-542-3123); and the New Mexico Department of Tourism, Lamy Building, Room 106, 491 Old Santa Fe Trail, Santa Fe, NM 87503 (800-545-2040 or 505-827-7400).

We list events held in Arizona and New Mexico separately by state, in chronological order as much as possible. (For Arizona, several events held just over the border in California, New Mexico, or Utah are also included.) Hopi events are not listed. However, the Hopi ceremonial calendar is very rich. Katsina ceremonies begin in late December and end during July. The non-katsina events take place during the rest of the year. Each village schedules its ceremonies individually. For information as to when ceremonial or other events take place and whether they are open to the public, contact the Hopi Tribal Council, P.O. Box 123, Kykotsmovi, AZ 86039, tel. 520-734-2441, ext. 100/101, or the various village community development offices: Bacavi 520-734-9360, Polacca 520-737-2670, Kykotsmovi 520-734-2474, Shungopavi 520-734-9278, Sipaulovi 520-737-2570, Moenkopi 520-283-6684, Hotevilla 520-734-2420, or the Hopi Civic Center at 520-734-6686.

Arizona (and Adjacent California, New Mexico, and Utah)

January	Havasupai Reservation; *Land Day.* Rex Tilousi, 520-448-2731.
January: *2nd Saturday*	Ak-Chin Reservation; *Annual Election Barbecue.* Carole Lopez, 520-568-9480.
February: *1st weekend*	Tohono O'odham Reservation at Sells, AZ; *Annual Rodeo and Fair.* Silas Hendricks, Jerilyn Norris 520-383-2221, ext. 228.

February: *2nd week*	East Cocopah Reservation; *Powwow.* Tribal Admin. Office, 520-627-2102.
February: *3rd Saturday*	Gila River Reservation at Sacaton, AZ; *Ira Hayes Memorial Day.* Rebecca Nelson, 520-418-3661.
February: *end*	Camp Verde Reservation; *Exodus Day.* Ernestine Larson, 520-567-3649.
February or March	Gila River Reservation at Sacaton, AZ; *Mul-chu-tha Tribal Fair.* Yvette Jackson, 520-562-3311.
March	Fort Yuma Reservation; *Powwow.* Quechan Tribal Council, P.O. Box 1352, Yuma, AZ 85364, 619-572-0213.
March 3	Colorado River Reservation at Manataba Park; *CRIT Heritage Day.* Betty L. Cornelius, 520-669-9211.
March: *1st Sunday*	Gila River Reservation at Laveen, AZ; *St. John's Festival.* Brother Austin, 520-550-2400.
Easter: *varies with date of holiday*	Pascua Yaqui Reservation; *Easter Ceremonies: Fiesta on Saturday Before Palm Sunday; Holy Week.* Anselmo Valencia Tori, Pascua Yaqui Tribe of Arizona, 7474 South Camino de Oeste, Tucson, AZ 85746, 520-883-5001.
Easter: *varies with date of holiday*	At Barrio Libre south of Tucson, and at Guadalupe near Phoenix, AZ; *Holy Week and Easter Celebrations: Solo and Group Dance Performances, Animal Representations, etc.* Anselmo Valencia Tori, Pascua Yaqui Tribe of Arizona, 7474 South Camino de Oeste, Tucson, AZ 85746, 520-883-5001.
April	Fort Apache Reservation at Canyon Day, AZ; *Canyon Day Open Show.* Noland Clay, 520-338-1764.
April	Fort McDowell Reservation; *Powwow.* Colleen Stacey, 602-837-2358.
April	Gila River Reservation; *Rodeo and Miss Gila River Pageant.* Gila River Community Council, P.O. Box 97, Sacaton, AZ 85247, 520-562-3311.
April	Navajo Reservation at Tsaile, AZ; *Annual Navajo Community College Powwow Celebration.* Walter Jensen, 520-724-6600.
April	San Carlos Reservation at Bylas, AZ; *Mt. Turnbull Celebration.* Angeline Moses, 520-475-2361.
April: *2nd Saturday*	Ak-Chin Reservation in Him-Dak Museum; *Ak-Chin Him-Dak Anniversary Celebration.* Him-Dak Museum staff, 520-568-9480.

April 15   Cocopah Reservation; *Cocopa Land Acquisition.* William Wachunas, 520-627-2102.

Spring: San Carlos Reservation at San Carlos, AZ; *Spring*
call for date *Roundup Rodeo.* Josephine Haozous or Rose Rope, 520-475-2361.

April through Fort Apache Reservation at various locations; *Sunrise*
September   *Dance Ceremony.* Tribal Council Secretary, 520-338-4346.

April through San Carlos Reservation; *Sunrise Dances.* Josephine
October   Haozous or Rose Rope, 520-475-2361.

May   Fort Apache Reservation at Cibecue, AZ; *Junior Rodeo.* Judy deHose, 520-332-2488.

May   Fort Apache Reservation at Whiteriver, AZ; *Headstart Rodeo and Parade.* Elaine Burnside, 520-338-4938.

May   Hualapai Reservation at Peach Springs, AZ; *Route 66 Days.* Dallas Quasula, 520-769-2216.

May   Salt River Reservation; *Senior Citizens Bazaar.* Evalyn Burns, 602-874-8427.

June   Hualapai Reservation at Peach Springs, AZ; *Sobriety Festival.* Hualapai Sobriety Festival Committee, 520-769-2216.

June   Navajo Reservation at Tsaile, AZ; *Annual Native American Music Festival.* Ferlin Clark, 520-724-6817, Walter Jensen, 520-724-6743, or Lori Lee, 520-871-2582.

June   San Carlos Reservation at San Carlos, AZ; *June 18 Celebration.* Josephine Haozous or Rose Rope, 520-475-2361.

Summer   Camp Verde Reservation; *Powwow.* Pauline Jackson, 520-567-5355, or Yavapai-Apache Community Council, P.O. Box 1188, Camp Verde, AZ 86322, 520-567-3649.

Summer   Yavapai-Prescott Reservation; *Intertribal Powwow.* Yavapai-Prescott Board of Directors, 530 E. Merritt, Prescott, AZ 86301-2038, 520-445-8790.

July   Fort Apache Reservation at Canyon Day, AZ; *All-Indian Rodeo.* Noland Clay, 520-338-1764.

July   Navajo Reservation at Crownpoint, NM; *Annual Eastern Navajo Fair.* 505-786-6159/6160.

July 1–4   Colorado River Reservation at Manataba Park; *4th of July.* Gary Short, 520-669-9652.

July 1–4	Colorado River Reservation at Manataba Park; *Miss Junior Miss* and *Little Miss CRIT Pageants.* Amanda Soliz, 520-669-9211.
July 4	Ak-Chin Reservation; *4th of July Fireworks and Picnic.* Bill White, 520-568-2258.
July 4	Navajo Reservation at Window Rock, AZ; *Fourth of July Celebration.* Leo Watchman, Jr., 520-871-6478.
August: 2nd week	Havasupai Reservation; *Peach Festival.* Rex Tilousi, 520-448-2731.
August	Fort Apache Reservation at Cibecue, AZ; *"Old-timers" Junior Rodeo.* Vangie Gatewood, 520-332-2535.
August	Hualapai Reservation at Peach Springs, AZ; *Miss Hualapai Pageant.* Hualapai Pageant Committee, 520-769-2216.
August	Navajo Reservation at Chinle, AZ; *Central Navajo Fair.* Roselyn Yazzi, 520-674-3611/3614.
September	Havasupai Reservation; *Indian Day.* Don Watahomigie, 520-448-2901, or Havasupai Tribal Council, P.O. Box 10, Supai, AZ 86435, 520-448-2961.
September	Navajo Reservation at Bluff, UT; *Utah Navajo Fair: Rodeo, Powwow, Dance.* 801-672-2381.
September	Navajo Reservation at Dilkon, AZ; *Southwestern Navajo Fair.* Jerry Freddy, 520-657-3376/9244.
September	Navajo Reservation at Ramah, NM; *Annual Ramah Community Fair.* 505-775-3256/3257/3258.
September	Navajo Reservation at Window Rock, AZ; *Navajo Nation Annual Fair, Rodeo, and Powwow.* Leo Watchman, Jr., 520-871-6478/7310.
September: Labor Day weekend	Fort Apache Reservation at Whiteriver, AZ; *Tribal Fair and Rodeo.* Fair Commission, 520-338-4346, or White Mountain Apache Tribal Council, P.O. Box 700, Whiteriver, AZ 85941, 520-338-4346.
September: 3rd weekend	Colorado River Reservation at Manataba Park; *Miss Indian Arizona Pageant.* Sandra Dick, Vicki Laffoon, 520-669-9211.
September: 3rd weekend	Colorado River Reservation at Manataba Park; *National Indian Days Celebration.* Valerie Welsh, 520-669-9211.
September: last Friday	Hualapai Reservation at Peach Springs, AZ; *Indian Day.* Recreation Office, 520-769-2216, or Hualapai

	Tribal Council, P.O. Box 179, Peach Springs, AZ 86434, 520-769-2216.
September: *last Friday*	Cocopah Reservation; *Indian Recognition Day.* William Wachunas, 520-627-2102, or Cocopah Tribal Council, P.O. Bin G, Somerton, AZ 85350.
October	Navajo Reservation at Shiprock, NM; *Northern Navajo Fair.* Sally Begay, 505-368-5312/5321.
October	Navajo Reservation at Tuba City, AZ; *Western Navajo Fair.* Mary Maloney, 520-283-5782.
October	Salt River Reservation; *Junior Miss Salt River Pageant.* Sarah Makil, 602-874-8000.
October	Salt River Reservation; *Miss Salt River Pageant.* Dorine Andrews, 602-874-8000.
October	San Xavier Reservation; *Miss Tohono O'odham Pageant.* Tohono O'odham Council, P.O. Box 837, Sells, AZ 85634, 520-383-2221.
October 4	Ak-Chin Reservation, St. Francis Catholic Church; *Ak-Chin St. Francis Church Feast.* Leona Kakar, 520-568-2227, or Ak-Chin Indian Community, 42507 West Peters and Nall Road, Maricopa, AZ 85239, 520-568-2618.
October: *mid-month*	Fort Mohave Reservation at Needles, CA; *Fort Mojave Indian Days.* Iris Jackson, 619-326-4810.
October: *mid-month*	Fort Mohave Reservation at Needles, CA; *Miss Fort Mojave Pageant.* Melba Guerrero, 619-326-4591.
October: *mid-month*	Fort Mohave Reservation at Needles, CA; *Fort Mohave Spirit Run.* Victor Van Fleet, 619-326-4591, or Fort Mojave Indian Tribe, 500 Merriman Avenue, Needles, CA 92363, 619-326-4591.
October: *late*	Tohono O'odham Reservation at Sells, AZ; *Rodeo and Fair.* Silas Hendricks, 520-383-2221, ext. 228.
November	Fort McDowell Reservation; *Powwow Trail of Tears.* Fort McDowell Mohave-Apache Indian Community, P.O. Box 17779, Fountain Hills, AZ 85269, 602-837-5121.
November	Gila River Reservation at Babchule, AZ; *Arts and Crafts Native American Dance Festival.* John Long, 520-315-3411, or Gila River Community Council, P.O. Box 97, Sacaton, AZ 85247, 520-562-3311.

November	Salt River Reservation; *Red Mountain Eagle Powwow.* Salt River Pima-Maricopa Indian Community Council, Route 1, Box 216, Scottsdale, AZ 85256, 602-941-7277.
November	San Carlos Reservation at San Carlos, AZ; *Miss San Carlos Pageant.* Josephine Haozous or Rose Rope, 520-475-2361.
November	San Carlos Reservation at San Carlos, AZ; *Rodeo Queen Pageant.* Josephine Haozous or Rose Rope, 520-475-2361, or San Carlos Apache Tribal Council, P.O. Box 0, San Carlos, AZ 85550, 520-475-2361.
November	San Carlos Reservation at San Carlos, AZ; *San Carlos Veterans Memorial Parade, Rodeo, and Powwow.* Josephine Haozous or Rose Rope, 520-475-2361.
November: 1st week	Fort McDowell Reservation; *Orme Victory Celebration.* Colleen Stacey, 602-837-2358.
December	Colorado River Reservation on Indian rodeo grounds; *All-Indian Rodeo (Parker Indian Rodeo Association).* Roy Leivas, 520-669-2121, or Colorado River Indian Tribes, Route 1, Box 23-B, Parker, AZ 85334, 520-669-9211.
December	Navajo Reservation at Window Rock, AZ; *Navajo Nation Arts and Crafts Fair.* Irving Nelson, 520-871-7303.
December	San Xavier Reservation; *San Francis Xavier Celebration.* Tohono O'odham Council, P.O. Box 837, Sells, AZ 85634, 520-383-2221.
Monthly	Navajo Reservation at Crownpoint, NM; *Navajo Rug Auction.* Ena Chavez, 505-786-5302, or Navajo Tourism Department, P.O. Box 663, Window Rock, AZ 86515, 520-871-6659/6436/7371.
Call for date	Tonto Apache Reservation; *Mazatzal Casino.* Sue Dolan, 1-800-777-PLAY or 520-474-6044, or Tonto Apache Tribal Council, Tonto Apache Reservation 30, Payson, AZ 85541, 520-474-5000.
Call for date	Fort McDowell Reservation; *Culture Festival of Arts and Crafts.* Robert Kingsley, 602-837-1424, or Fort McDowell Mohave-Apache Indian Community, P.O. Box 17779, Fountain Hills, AZ 85269, 602-837-5121.

New Mexico

January 1	Plaza of Jemez Pueblo; *Animal or Matachina Dances.* Director of Tourism, Pueblo of Jemez Department of Tourism, P.O. Box 100, Jemez Pueblo, NM 87024, 505-834-7235.
January 1	Taos Pueblo; *Taos Turtle Dance.* Taos Pueblo, P.O. Box 1846, Taos, NM 87571, 505-758-9593.
January 6	Taos Pueblo; *Kings' Day: Traditional Animal Dances.* Taos Pueblo, P.O. Box 1846, Taos, NM 87571, 505-758-9593.
January 6 and 7	Jemez Pueblo; *Three Kings' Day, Buffalo and Animal Dances.* Director of Tourism, Pueblo of Jemez Department of Tourism, P.O. Box 100, Jemez Pueblo, NM 87024, 505-834-7235.
January: *beginning*	Isleta Pueblo; *Corn, Turtle, and Other Dances.* 505-869-3111.
January: *beginning*	San Ildefonso Pueblo; *Eagle Dance.* 505-455-2273.
January 6	Laguna Pueblo: all six villages (Encinal, Laguna, Mesita, Paguate, Paraje, and Seama); *Feast of the Three Kings.* Office of the Governor, Pueblo of Laguna, P.O. Box 194, Laguna, NM 87026, 505-552-6654.
January 22 and 23	San Ildefonso Pueblo; *San Ildefonso Pueblo Feast Day: Comanche, Buffalo, and Deer Dances.* 505-455-2273.
January 25	Picuris Pueblo; *St. Paul's Feast Day.* 505-587-2519.
February	Acoma "Sky City"; *Governor's Feast.* Acoma Tourist Center, P.O. Box 309, Acoma, NM 87034, 505-470-4966.
February: *beginning*	Picuris Pueblo; *Various Dances.* 505-587-2519.
February: *2nd week*	San Juan Pueblo; *Deer Dance.* 505-852-4400.
February: *late*	Isleta Pueblo; *Evergreen Dance.* 505-869-3111.
March 19	Laguna Pueblo: Old Laguna Village; *St. Joseph's Feast Day (original): Dances.* Office of the Governor, Pueblo of Laguna, P.O. Box 194, Laguna, NM 87026, 505-552-6654.

Easter	Jemez Pueblo; *Corn Dances.* Director of Tourism, Pueblo of Jemez Department of Tourism, P.O. Box 100, Jemez Pueblo, NM 87024, 505-834-7235.
Easter Sunday	Zia Pueblo; *Easter Sunday.* Pueblo of Zia, 135 Capitol Square Drive, Zia Pueblo, NM 87053-6013, 505-867-3304.
April 1 through October 15, *weekends*	Jemez Red Rocks, Jemez Pueblo; *Jemez Pueblo Open-Air Market.* Director of Tourism, Pueblo of Jemez Department of Tourism, P.O. Box 100, Jemez Pueblo, NM 87024, 505-834-7235.
May: *beginning*	Taos Pueblo; *Santa Cruz Feast Day: Corn Dance, Foot Races.* Taos Pueblo, P.O. Box 1846, Taos, NM 87571, 505-758-9593.
May 1	Pueblo of San Felipe; *St. Philip's Day Celebration.* Pueblo de San Felipe, P.O. Box 4339, San Felipe Pueblo, NM 87001, 505-867-3381.
May: *1st Sunday*	McCartys, NM; *May Celebrations.* 505-552-6604.
May 14	Taos Pueblo; *San Ysidro Fiesta (blessing of the fields).* Taos Pueblo, P.O. Box 1846, Taos, NM 87571, 505-758-9593.
June: *2nd weekend*	Jemez Red Rocks, Jemez Pueblo; *Annual Towa Arts and Crafts Show.* Director of Tourism, Pueblo of Jemez Department of Tourism, P.O. Box 100, Jemez Pueblo, NM 87024, 505-834-7235.
June 13	Sandia Pueblo; *Sandia Feast Day: Corn Dance.* 505-867-3317.
June 13	San Ildefonso Pueblo; *St. Anthony's Feast Day.* 505-455-2273.
June 13	San Juan Pueblo; *St. Anthony's Feast Day: Dances.* 505-852-4400.
June 13	Santa Clara Pueblo; *Saint Anthony's Feast Day.* Santa Clara Pueblo Tourism Department, P.O. Box 580, Espanola, NM 87532, 505-753-7326.
June 13	Taos Pueblo; *St. Anthony Feast Day: Traditional Men's and Women's Dances.* Taos Pueblo, P.O. Box 1846, Taos, NM 87571, 505-758-9593.

June 23–24	San Juan Pueblo; *San Juan Pueblo Feast Day: Buffalo and Comanche Dances; Foot Races; Arts and Crafts.* 505-852-4400.
June 24	Isleta Pueblo; *San Juan's Day: Dances.* 505-869-3111.
June 29	Isleta Pueblo; *San Pedro's Day: Rooster Pull.* 505-869-3111.
June: end	Taos Pueblo; *San Juan Feast Day: Traditional Dances.* Taos Pueblo, P.O. Box 1846, Taos, NM 87571, 505-758-9593.
July: beginning	Picuris Pueblo; *Weekend High Country Arts and Crafts Festival.* 505-587-2519.
July 4	Nambe Pueblo; *Nambe Falls Celebration: Special Events and Dances.* 505-455-2036.
July 4 weekend	Mescalero Apache Ceremonial Grounds and Sam Miller Rodeo Arena at Mescalero, NM; *Tribal Ceremonial and Rodeo.* Mescalero Apache Tribe, P.O. Box 227, Mescalero, NM 88340, 505-671-4494, or Mescalero Apache Nation, P.O. Box 176, Mescalero, NM 88340, 505-671-4495.
July 14	Cochiti Pueblo; *San Bonaventura Feast Day: Corn Dance.* 505-465-2244.
July: mid-month	Taos Pueblo; *Powwow.* Taos Pueblo, P.O. Box 1846, Taos, NM 87571, 505-758-9593.
July: second half	Santa Clara Pueblo; *Eight Northern Indian Pueblo Council: Arts and Crafts Show.* ENIPC Planning Office, 505-852-4265.
July 25	Cochiti Pueblo; *Santiago's Feast Day.* 505-465-2244.
July 25	Santo Domingo Pueblo; *Santiago's Feast Day.* 505-465-2214.
July 25–26	San Ildefonso Pueblo; *Santiago's Day: Various Dances.* 505-455-2273.
July 25–26	Santa Ana Pueblo; *Santiago Day and Santa Ana Feast Day: Dances.* 505-867-3301.
July 25–26	Taos Pueblo; *Santiago and Santa Ana Feast Days: Traditional Dances.* Taos Pueblo, P.O. Box 1846, Taos, NM 87571, 505-758-9593.
July 26	Laguna Pueblo: Seama Village; *St. Ann's Feast Day: Dances.* Office of the Governor, Pueblo of Laguna, P.O. Box 194, Laguna, NM 87026, 505-552-6654.

August: early   Pojoaque Pueblo; *Appreciation Day.* 505-455-2278.

August 2   Plaza of Jemez Pueblo; *St. Persingula Feast Day, Old Pecos Bull Ceremony, Corn Dances.* Director of Tourism, Pueblo of Jemez Department of Tourism, P.O. Box 100, Jemez Pueblo, NM 87024, 505-834-7235.

August 4   Santo Domingo Pueblo; *Santo Domingo Feast Day: Corn Dance.* 505-465-2214.

August 9–10   Picuris Pueblo; *San Lorenzo Feast Day: Dances, Pole Climbing, Traditional Foot Races, Arts and Crafts.* 505-587-2519.

August 10   Acomita, NM; *San Lorenzo Day: Corn Dance.* 505-552-6604.

August 12   Santa Clara Pueblo; *Santa Clara Feast Day: Dances.* Santa Clara Pueblo Tourism Department, P.O. Box 580, Espanola, NM 87532, 505-753-7326.

August 15   Laguna Pueblo: Mesita Village; *Assumption of Our Blessed Mother's Feast Day: Dances.* Office of the Governor, Pueblo of Laguna, P.O. Box 194, Laguna, NM 87026, 505-552-6654.

August: mid-month   Zia Pueblo; *Annual Fiesta: Dances.* Pueblo of Zia, 135 Capitol Square Drive, Zia Pueblo, NM 87053-6013, 505-867-3304.

August 28   Isleta Pueblo; *Isleta Feast Day.* 505-869-3111.

August and September   San Ildefonso Pueblo; *Corn Dances.* 505-455-2273.

September: beginning   Isleta Pueblo; *Harvest Dance.* 505-869-3111.

September: beginning   Santo Domingo Pueblo; *Arts and Crafts Fair.* 505-465-2214.

September 2   Acoma "Sky City"; *St. Estevan Feast Day: Dances.* 505-470-4966.

September 8   Laguna Pueblo: Encinal Village; *Nativity of the Blessed Virgin Mary's Feast Day: Harvest and Various Other Dances.* Office of the Governor, Pueblo of Laguna, P.O. Box 194, Laguna, NM 87026, 505-552-6654.

September 19   Laguna Pueblo: Old Laguna Village; *St. Joseph's Feast Day: Harvest and Various Other Dances.* Office of the Governor, Pueblo of Laguna, P.O. Box 194, Laguna, NM 87026, 505-552-6654.

September 25　Laguna Pueblo: Paguate Village; *St. Elizabeth's Feast Day: Harvest and Various Other Dances.* Office of the Governor, Pueblo of Laguna, P.O. Box 194, Laguna, NM 87026, 505-552-6654.

September 29–30　Taos Pueblo; *Vespers and Sundown Dance; San Geronimo Feast Day: Foot Races, Open-Air Market, Pole Climbing, Dances.* Taos Pueblo, P.O. Box 1846, Taos, NM 87571, 505-758-9593.

October: 1st and 2nd weekends　Jemez Red Rocks, Jemez Pueblo; *Fall Art Fiesta.* Director of Tourism, Pueblo of Jemez Department of Tourism, P.O. Box 100, Jemez Pueblo, NM 87024, 505-834-7235.

October 3–4　Nambe Pueblo; *St. Francis of Assisi Feast Day: Dances, Arts and Crafts.* 505-455-2036.

October 17　Laguna Pueblo: Paraje Village; *St. Margaret Mary's Feast Day: Harvest and Various Other Dances.* Office of the Governor, Pueblo of Laguna, P.O. Box 194, Laguna, NM 87026, 505-552-6654.

November 12　Plaza of Jemez Pueblo; *San Diego Feast Day: Corn Dances.* Director of Tourism, Pueblo of Jemez Department of Tourism, P.O. Box 100, Jemez Pueblo, NM 87024, 505-834-7235.

November 12　Tesuque Pueblo; *San Diego Feast Day: Dances.* 505-983-2667.

December: 1st weekend　Jemez Pueblo Civic Center; *Walatowa Winter Arts and Crafts Show.* Director of Tourism, Pueblo of Jemez Department of Tourism, P.O. Box 100, Jemez Pueblo, NM 87024, 505-834-7235.

December 12　Isleta Pueblo; *Guadalupe Day: Gift Throwing.* 505-869-3111.

December 12　Pojoaque Pueblo; *Guadalupe Feast Day: Dances, Arts and Crafts.* 505-455-2278.

December 12　Tesuque Pueblo; *Flag, Deer, and Buffalo Dances.* 505-983-2667.

December 24　Laguna Pueblo: Old Laguna Village; *Midnight Mass; Harvest, Arrow, Deer, and various other dances.* Office of the Governor, Pueblo of Laguna, P.O. Box 194, Laguna, NM 87026, 505-552-6654.

December 25　San Ildefonso Pueblo; *Matachinas and Various Dances.* 505-455-2273.

December 25	Taos Pueblo; *Matachina or Deer Dance*. Taos Pueblo, P.O. Box 1846, Taos, NM 87571, 505-758-9593.
December 25–28	Zia Pueblo; *Christmas*. Pueblo of Zia, 135 Capitol Square Drive, Zia Pueblo, NM 87053-6013, 505-867-3304.
December 26	San Juan Pueblo; *Turtle Dance*. 505-852-4400.
December 25–28	Laguna Pueblo: all six villages (Encinal, Laguna, Mesita, Paguate, Paraje, and Seama); *Christmas Day: dancing usually continues for three more days*. Office of the Governor, Pueblo of Laguna, P.O. Box 194, Laguna, NM 87026, 505-552-6654.
December 26–28	Acoma "Sky City"; *December Celebration*. 505-470-4966.

TO LEARN MORE

Thousands of popular and scholarly articles and books have been written about the Native Americans of the Southwest, and any selection of titles is necessarily limited and arbitrary. We list here primarily those works that are nontechnical and are usually to be found in the Southwest's museum and visitor center gift shops. Readers interested in further in-depth reading on these subjects can consult the subject catalogs of college or university libraries.

Adair, John. *The Navajo and Pueblo Silversmiths*. Norman: University of Oklahoma Press, 1944.

Adams, E. Charles. *The Origin and Development of the Pueblo Katsina Cult*. Tucson: University of Arizona Press, 1991.

Allen, Laura Graves. *Contemporary Hopi Pottery*. Flagstaff: Museum of Northern Arizona, 1984.

Bahti, Tom. *Southwestern Indian Tribes*. Las Vegas, NV: KC Publications, 1968.

Benedek, Emily. *Beyond the Four Corners of the World*: *A Navajo Woman's Journey*. New York: Alfred A. Knopf, 1995.

Blomberg, Nancy J. *Navajo Textiles*: *The William Randolph Hearst Collection*. Tucson: University of Arizona Press, 1988.

Bradfield, Richard Maitland. *An Interpretation of Hopi Culture*. Derby, England, 1995.

Chapman, Kenneth M. *Pueblo Pottery Designs*. New York: Dover Publications, 1995.

Colton, Harold S. *Hopi Kachina Dolls with a Key to Their Identification* (rev. ed.). Albuquerque: University of New Mexico Press, 1959.

Crown, Patricia L., and W. James Judge (eds.). *Chaco and Hohokam*: *Prehistoric Regional Systems in the American Southwest*. Santa Fe, NM: School of American Research Press, 1991.

Dedera, Don. *Artistry in Clay*: *Contemporary Pottery of the Southwest*. Flagstaff, AZ: Northland Press, 1985.

Dedera, Don. *Navajo Rugs*: *How to Find, Evaluate, Buy and Care for Them* (2d ed., rev.). Flagstaff, AZ: Northland Publishing, 1996.

Dittert, Alfred E., Jr., and Fred Plog. *Generations in Clay: Pueblo Pottery of the American Southwest.* Flagstaff, AZ: Northland Publishing, 1980.

Dutton, Bertha P. *American Indians of the Southwest* (rev. and enl. ed.). Albuquerque: University of New Mexico Press, 1983.

Gilpin, Laura. *The Enduring Navaho.* Austin: University of Texas Press, 1974.

Harlow, Francis H. *Modern Pueblo Pottery, 1880–1960.* Flagstaff, AZ: Northland Press, 1977.

Hayes, Allan, and John Blom. *Southwestern Pottery: Anasazi to Zuni.* Flagstaff, AZ: Northland Publishing, 1996.

Iliff, Flora Gregg. *People of the Blue Water: A Record of Life Among the Walapai and Havasupai Indians.* [1901]. Tucson: University of Arizona Press, 1954.

Jacka, Lois Essary. *Navajo Jewelry: A Legacy of Silver and Stone.* Flagstaff, AZ: Northland Publishing, 1995.

James, Harry C. *Pages from Hopi History.* Tucson: University of Arizona Press, 1974.

Kluckhohn, Clyde, and Dorothea Leighton. *The Navaho* (rev. ed.). Garden City, NY: Doubleday, 1962.

Leach, Nicky J. *The Guide to National Parks of the Southwest.* Tucson, AZ: Southwest Parks and Monuments Association, 1992.

Left Handed, Son of Old Man Hat: A Navajo Autobiography. [1938]. Recorded by Walter Dyk. Lincoln: University of Nebraska Press, 1966.

Lister, Robert H., and Florence C. Lister. *Those Who Came Before* (2d ed.). Tucson, AZ: Southwest Parks and Monuments Association, 1993.

Loftin, John D. *Religion and Hopi Life in the Twentieth Century.* Bloomington: Indiana University Press, 1991.

Mays, Buddy. *Indian Villages of the Southwest: A Practical Guide to the Pueblo Indian Villages of New Mexico and Arizona.* San Francisco: Chronicle Books, 1985.

Mesa Verde, Canyon de Chelly and Hovenweep. Casper, WY: World-Wide Research and Publishing Company, 1987.

Noble, David Grant. *Ancient Ruins of the Southwest: An Archaeological Guide* (rev. and enl. ed.). Flagstaff, AZ: Northland Publishing, 1991.

Polingaysi Qoyawayma (Elizabeth Q. White; as told to Vada F. Carlson). *No Turning Back: A Hopi Indian Woman's Struggle to Live in Two Worlds.* Albuquerque: University of New Mexico Press, 1964.

Roberts, David. *In Search of the Old Ones: Exploring the Anasazi World of the Southwest.* New York: Simon and Schuster, 1996.

Rodee, Marian E. *One Hundred Years of Navajo Rugs*. Albuquerque: University of New Mexico Press, 1995.

Rodee, Marian, and James Ostler. *Zuni Pottery*. Atglen, PA: Schiffer Publishing, 1986.

Sides, Dorothy Smith. *Decorative Art of the Southwestern Indians: 290 Copyright-Free Design Motifs for Artists and Craftsmen*. New York: Dover Publications, 1961.

Simmons, Leo W. (ed.). *Sun Chief: The Autobiography of a Hopi Indian*. New Haven, CT: Yale University Press, 1942.

Strutin, Michele. *Chaco: A Cultural Legacy*. Tucson, AZ: Southwest Parks and Monuments Association, 1994.

Tanner, Clara Lee. *Southwest Indian Craft Arts*. Tucson: University of Arizona Press, 1968.

Tanner, Clara Lee. *Indian Baskets of the Southwest*. Tucson: University of Arizona Press, 1983.

Tanner, Clara Lee (ed.). *Indian Arts and Crafts*. Phoenix: Arizona Highways, 1976.

Teiwes, Helga. *Hopi Basket Weaving: Artistry in Natural Fibers*. Tucson: University of Arizona Press, 1996.

Trimble, Stephen. *The People: Indians of the American Southwest*. Santa Fe, NM: School of American Research Press, 1993.

Trimble, Stephen. *Talking with the Clay: The Art of Pueblo Pottery*. Santa Fe, NM: School of American Research Press, 1993.

Viele, Catherine W. *Navajo National Monument*. Tucson, AZ: Southwest Parks and Monuments Association, 1993.

Walker, Steven L. *Indian Cultures of the American Southwest*. Scottsdale, AZ: Camelback Design Group and Canyonlands Publications, 1994.

Waters, Frank. *Book of the Hopi*. New York: Penguin Books, 1963.

Weber, Steven A., and P. David Seaman (eds.). *Havasupai Habitat: A. F. Whiting's Ethnography of a Traditional Indian Culture*. Tucson: University of Arizona Press, 1985.

Wright, Barton. *Hopi Kachinas: The Complete Guide to Collecting Kachina Dolls*. Flagstaff, AZ: Northland Publishing, 1977.

Wright, Barton. *Clowns of the Hopi: Tradition Keepers and Delight Makers*. Flagstaff, AZ: Northland Publishing, 1994.

ABOUT THE BOOK AND AUTHORS

This guide to the Native Americans of the Southwest is a concise but comprehensive introduction that gives readers a sound anthropological and historical background of the area and fosters an appreciation of the Native American peoples who make the Southwest their home. The authors offer individual sections on the main prehistoric and contemporary peoples of the region, describing their ways of life, their art, and their cultural monuments.

For those eager to see at least some of these cultural monuments and to learn about Native American cultures, this book serves as a guide to the most memorable sites in Arizona, New Mexico, Colorado, and Utah. In addition, the authors provide a comprehensive list of museums and a calendar of tribal events that are open to interested visitors: rodeos, fairs, dances, festivals, and the like. Several maps are also included to assist the visitor in locating the sites discussed in the book.

Zdenek (Denny) Salzmann is professor emeritus of anthropology at the University of Massachusetts at Amherst and adjunct professor at Northern Arizona University. **Joy M. Salzmann** has taught English at the college and secondary school levels and has collaborated with her husband on his many publications. The Salzmanns live in the beauty of the red rock country near Sedona, Arizona.

INDEX

In addition to abbreviations for states (AZ, CO, NM, NV, TX, and UT), the following are used below: NaMo, NHP, and NP, for National Monument, National Historic(al) Park, and National Park, respectively. Museums and exhibits listed in Appendix A are indexed according to locality, and events listed in Appendix B according to type (dances, feast days, rodeos, etc.).

151